Vol.16
Gresley V1/V3 & Thompson L1 classes

Vol.21
Class A5 to A8, H1, H2, L1(L3), L2, M1 & M2 Tank Engines

Class N1 & N2 Tank Engines

Vol.17
Class B13, B14, B15 & B16 - The NE 4-6-0's

Vol.22
Class B1 (B18) to B9 - The GCR 4-6-0's

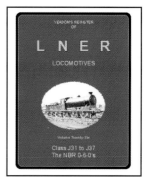

Vol.26
Class J31 to J37 - The NBR 0-6-0's

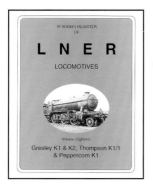

Vol.18
Gresley K1 & K2, Thompson K1/1 and Peppercorn K1

Vol.23
Q5, Q6, Q7 & Q10 - The NER 0-8-0's

Vol.27
Class N7 Tank Engines

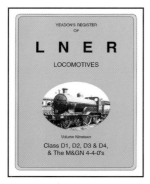

Vol.19
Class D1 to D4 & the M&GN 4-4-0's

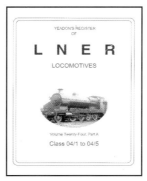

Vol.24A
Class O4 Parts 1 to 5

Vol.28
R1, S1, T1 & the WM&CQ 0-8-0 - The Pre-Group Eight-Coupled tanks.

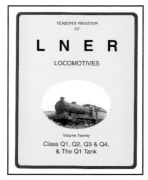

Vol.20
Class Q1 to Q4 & the Q1 Tank Engines

Vol.24B
Class O4 Parts 6 to 8, O5 & the Thompson O1

Vol.29
Class D5 to D12 - the GCR 4-4-0's

YEADON'S REGISTER

of

L N E R

LOCOMOTIVES

Volume Twenty- Four B

**Class O4/6, O4/7, O4/8, O5
and Thompson O1**

Copyright Booklaw/Railbus 2002
ISBN 1 899624 57 0

YEADON'S REGISTER OF L.N.E.R. LOCOMOTIVES - VOLUME 24B

EDITOR'S NOTE & ACKNOWLEDGEMENTS

So, we come to Part B of Volume 24. Having accepted the first part with some enthusiasm, we hope that this part will also meet with your approval.

In this one we cover the remaining class parts of the O4's, the O5 class, and the erstwhile Thompson O1 2-8-0. The latter class was to have become the LNER standard 2-8-0 goods engine but time and other factors were against it and after 1948, British Railways saw no need for a 2-8-0 goods engine anyway, at least not a BR Standard type, there being a couple of thousand 2-8-0's already in existence of which half were fairly modern at that time. So, the Thompson O1, although still being rebuilt from various O4's into the early 1950's, had a somewhat shortened career and with dieselisation gaining pace the vast majority went for scrap in the early 1960's.

In a previous volume of this series we mentioned how many of the LNER locomotives we had reviewed at that time. In this volume we will not go into any numbers but it is worth mentioning that quite a few of the alphabetical locomotive type classifications used by the LNER have now been covered, the last two volumes alone have finished off the O and Q groups. However, there are many more to go - for instance, lots of D's, even more J's not to mention the numerous classes found in the E, F and G groups.

All the people mentioned in Part A of this volume contributed in some way to getting this particular Part finished also - thanks everybody.

It goes without saying that Annie, Jean and Simon get our thanks once again.

Hopefully the situation regarding the size of this volume should not crop up again so it now seems appropriate to thank all of you readers for supporting this two part work and of course the rest of the series of *Yeadon's Register of LNER Locomotives*.

The next Register, Volume 25, will feature the GNR 0-6-2T's of LNER classes N1 and N2.

The Yeadon Collection is available for inspection and anyone who wishes to
inspect it should contact:-
The Archivist
Brynmor Jones Library
University of Hull
Hull
HU6 7RX
Tel: 01482-465265
A catalogue of the Yeadon collection is available.

First published in the United Kingdom by
BOOKLAW/RAILBUS 2002 in association with CHALLENGER
382 Carlton Hill, Nottingham, NG4 1JA.
Printed and bound by The Amadeus Press, Cleckheaton, West Yorkshire.

INTRODUCTION

Part B of this volume carries on from where Part A finished, at Part 6 of Class O4. The initial Introduction of the O4 class in general will be found in Part A of Volume 24. The index contained within this part coincides with that found in Part A except that the engines contained within this part are set out in bold type whereas those in Part B are in normal type. This part in particular contains all the tables appertaining to Class O5 and the Thompson O1's also within this part are the tables for the O4 class from No.6535 onwards. All the O4's preceding that engine are set out in Part A.

To recap on the presentation of the O4 class in Volume 24, it will be seen that the tables are laid out in the order of GC/LNER numbering rather than in the order of building.

Photographic coverage in this volume starts with those engines of O4 Part 6 and carries on into Part 7 and 8. These are followed by Class O5 and the Thompson O1 class.

O4/6

In December 1938 the separate classification O4 Part 6 was introduced to cover the conversions from Class O5 - previously they had been included with O4 Part 1. These conversions entailed fitting a conventional O4 boiler in place of the 5ft 6in. boiler on the O5's. However, the original cabs (including those with double side window fitted to the last five to be built, Nos.5014, 5015, 5017, 5019 and 5022) had been retained. These were larger in overall height, and at the eves, than the normal O4 cab and were thus outside the LNER Composite Load Gauge. At the time of the introduction of the O4/6 classification, the programme of reduction of chimney and dome height on Class O4 was nearly complete so it became necessary to distinguish the ex-O5 engines as still not within the all line gauge because of their cab dimensions, hence the new classification O4/6.

The first conversion to O4 took place in 1922 when two of the class (Nos.412 and 413) were rebuilt by the GCR. One further conversion was carried out by the LNER in 1926 whilst eleven more were done in the 1930's. All these were reclassified from O4/1 to O4/6 in December 1938.

With the likelihood of war breaking out, it was decided in 1939 to cut down the cabs of Class O4/6 to suit the LNER gauge in order to widen their sphere of operation. No.5019 was the first to be dealt with, in May 1939, followed by the remainder during 1940-41.

During 1940-43 the five surviving O5 engines were also rebuilt to O4/6, the last being No.5422 in January 1943. These received altered cabs at the same time. When rebuilt in 1941, Nos.5420 (September) and 5421 (October) were sent straightaway to the Middle East - indeed out of the nineteen former O5 engines, no fewer than six went to the WD in 1941.

Two of the remaining O4/6's were rebuilt to Part 8, 63914 (ex-5012) in July 1955 and 63915 (ex-5013) in January 1956. The Part became extinct in June 1965 when 63913 (ex-5011) was withdrawn.

O4/7

1939 saw another class part of the O4's created by Gresley when a shorter version of the Diagram 15A boiler (*see* O4/5, Volume 24, Part A) was fitted to forty-three engines over the years up to 1947. These became Part 7 of Class O4. The new boiler (Diagram 15D) was built up to 1943 and forty-six were produced in total, including three spares. Before the last conversions took place Edward Thompson had introduced his Diagram 100A boiler, used on the B1's, onto the frames of the O4 class in an effort to standardise the LNER 2-8-0 classes and it is a mystery why further O4/7 conversions took place.

The Diagram 15D boiler allowed the retention of a GC pattern smokebox and avoided the expense of fitting a separate saddle as had been done on the O4/4 and O4/5 rebuilds. The new smokebox was the same diameter as on Class O5 although 11¾in. shorter. The chimney was one inch shorter than on previous Gresley rebuilds because the smokebox was of greater diameter than on these. The original cab was retained except for the frontplate and spectacle windows, revised to suit the round top firebox. Like the O4/5's, a blister was fabricated into the right hand side wall of the cab to make room for the rotation of the screw reversing handle, set further out due to the increase in the boiler diameter.

Gorton works naturally undertook most of the rebuilding to O4/7, but in 1942 Stratford became involved in the overhaul of Class O4 and this included the conversion of five engines to Class O4/7.

One O4/7 (63596) became an O1, six others became O4/8's whilst thirty-four of the original forty-three remained as O4/7's to withdrawal. The last was 63770 (ex-6584) which was condemned in December 1965 making O4 Part 7 extinct.

O4/8

This conversion was introduced in 1944 when No.6281 was rebuilt to O4/8 by the fitting of a Diagram 100A (LNER Standard) boiler but the actual Part was not introduced until 1946. Up to 1958 ninety-nine engines were converted to Part 8, these originating from all the other previous seven parts of the O4 class.

Besides the fitting of the standard boiler, a new side window cab was fitted and a new saddle was put onto the frames to accommodate the smokebox. The original cylinders were retained as was the motion. Apparently if the cylinders were found to be in poor condition then new B1 type cylinders would have been fitted and this would then have created a Class O1.

It is interesting to note that the LNER only converted sixteen O4's to Part 8 and most of those done by BR (70) were carried out between 1955 and 1958. Only thirteen had been created between 1952 (the first BR conversion) and 1954.

When the London Midland Region took over responsibility for Gorton works in 1958 it was decided that no more conversions would take place and Gorton then carried on with the repair of the existing members of Class O4 until its closure. Ironically, the last locomotive to receive a general overhaul at Gorton was another 2-8-0 type with a similar reputation to the O4's - though from a different designer - Stanier 8F No.48530. To add further irony, this London Midland engine was one of those built by the LNER at Doncaster during WW2 and loaned to the LNER until March 1947 whence it went to the London Midland & Scottish Railway, finally being withdrawn by BR in March 1966, not quite twenty-one years old - a mere youngster in O4 terms.

O4/6. Although not recognised as such until the December 1938 Diagram Book alterations, Part 6 had been created on 1st July 1922 when O5 class No.413 was ex works with a boiler from No.1243, followed on 11th August 1922 by No.412 with the boiler from No.353. The object was to enable two 5ft 6in. boilers to be used as spares for Classes O5 and B6. As Nos.412 and 413 retained tenders with water scoops, the LNER put them into Part 1 until it was realised they retained the original large cab which put them outside the 13ft 0in. load gauge.

O4/7. Part 7 was the third, last, and most successful Gresley application of the 5ft 6in. round top firebox boiler. Diagram 15D was based on the 15A but was 11⅞in. shorter in the barrel which permitted use of a GC style smokebox, needing no saddle. Starting with No.6241, ex works on 11th November 1939, Part 7 totalled forty-one before being stopped by Thompson's different ideas on rebuilding and reboilering O4 class. Part 7 was made from fourteen Part 1; two Part 2; twenty-four Part 3, and one Part 5. Gorton did the first twenty-four, Nos.5390, 6241 and 6353 in 1939; Nos.5350, 5378, 5391, 5405, 6209, 6223, 6248, 6258, 6300, 6319, 6352, 6540, 6573, 6584, 6586, 6612, 6621, 6633 in 1940 and Nos.5093, 6337, 6364 by April 1941. The next six, Nos.5335, 6211, 6249, 6318, 6358 and 6572 in May to September 1942 were done at Stratford, after which Gorton dealt with Nos.5353, 6277, 6291, 6295, 6516 and 6618 in 1943, and Nos.6276, 6286, 6305 and 6528 by 8th April 1944. Finally, Gorton changed No.3705 (ex 6320) from Part 5 as late as 6th December 1947. Gorton.

O4/8. Edward Thompson carried on the process of fitting 5ft 6in. diameter boilers with round top firebox to O4 class but using his Diagram 100A boiler as fitted on Class B1. Where cylinders did not need renewal, only the boiler, smokebox and cab were changed and the result was the creation of O4 Part 8. No.6281, ex works on 29th April 1944, was the first, and ten more were done in that same year: 5388, 6205, 6228, 6262, 6292, 6293, 6306, 6522, 6590 and 6609. Five more were done by the LNER in 1947 and then no others until 63750 in October and 63807 in November 1952. In each of the years 1953 to 1958 further conversions took place, the total being increased by eighty-one in those six years. Further work was then halted because the London Midland Region became responsible for Gorton works from 29th December 1958, so the full total for Part 8 was ninety-nine. Gorton, 1944.

O5. In March 1916, only 4½ years after the 2-8-0 type was introduced on the GCR, Robinson began the effort to put on a bigger boiler to give more steam to the 21in. cylinders. Two orders, each for ten, with 5ft 6in. boilers, were placed with Gorton but one of the first batch was made a 4-6-0 and became a B6 class. Nos.412 to 415, 417 to 422, and 10 to 13 were built from January 1918 to October 1919.

The O4/8's were in fact the last GC designed locomotives working on BR and when the final withdrawals were carried out in April 1966 they were amongst the last steam locomotives on the Eastern Region. To the end they were employed on coal trains, mainly in the Doncaster area, a job they were designed for and on which they performed so well for fifty-five years.

O5

The GCR Class 8M was essentially an 8K with a larger 5ft 6in. diameter boiler. Nineteen were built at Gorton between 1918 and 1921. Originally there was to have been twenty of these 2-8-0's but No.416 came out instead as a 4-6-0.

The Diagram 15B boiler used by the O5's was the same as the boiler used by the B6 4-6-0's and before conversion of the O5's to O4's, there was plenty of interchangeability between the two classes (see also Vol.22).

The cab of the O5 class was 7in. wider than the cab on the O4 but because of the nature of the boiler layout it was some 5in. shorter. The last five came out with double side windows offering a bit more protection to the enginemen.

In 1922 the GC rebuilt two of the class (5412 and 5413) to O4 standard, a start of things to come. It is probable that this initial rebuilding, coming so soon after construction, was done in order to create two spare boilers to allow rotation amongst Class O5 and the three engines of Class B6.

Five of this class were fitted from new with the distinctive battle-axe shaped balance weights on their driving wheels. A further engine got them in an exchange of wheels sets. A précis of the situation is as follows:-

5013 (3915) - changed to crescent pattern circa 1923.
5014 - withdrawn 1941.
5015 (3917) - to O4/6 June 1935.
5019 - withdrawn 1941.
5022 (63920) - to O4/6 October 1935.
5420 - probably exchanged wheel sets with 5013. Withdrawn in 1941.

Only two of the seventeen engines, Nos.5418 (14th February 1924) and 5421 (1st November 1924) went straight to full LNER number. It is assumed that four would get the C suffix, Nos.415c (29th September 1923), 420c (13th October 1923), 414c (24th November 1923) and 419c (16th January 1924). The other eleven had their first LNER general repair between March and August 1923. Nos.422 (10th March), 10 (14th April), 22 (21st April), 14 (9th June), 15 (23rd June), 19 (23rd June) and it is reasonable to assume these would get L&NER. Most likely Nos.17 (7th July), 11 (13th July), 417 (30th July), 12 (15th August) and 13 (25th August) would have just LNER. Only No.5421 would not have the large brass number-plate on the cab side. No.5417 ex works on 21st January 1926 still showed evidence of being so fitted.

In August 1926 the LNER started its programme of rebuilding the O5's to O4's and No.5012 was the first to become an O4 Part 1. The others eventually followed it but it was October 1932 before the next O5 (5017) was rebuilt. In January 1943 the rebuilding of the O5's was completed but during the interim period the LNER had decided to reclassify the rebuilds into their own sub class and they became O4 Part 6. BR took two of the class and rebuilt them yet again in the mid-1950's to Part 8 engines.

O1. **The heavy goods engine in Thompson's Standardisation Programme was based on rebuilding engines of Class O4 using their frames, wheels and tender, with the boiler, cylinders, valve gear, and cab as used on his Class B1 mixed traffic design. No.6595 was the first, ex Gorton on 12th February 1944.**

Thompson O1

The O1 class came about through the desire of Edward Thompson to create standardisation within the LNER motive power fleet.

Altogether, fifty-eight O4's were rebuilt to O1 between 1944 and 1949 - BR were responsible for only seven of those rebuilds, the rest being carried out by the LNER during the latter war years and the few years leading up to Nationalisation.

The boiler employed was the round-topped Diagram 100A as used successfully on the Thompson B1 engines which were rapidly becoming the LNER's Standard 4-6-0.

Apart from the original GC design tender and the 2-8-0 configured frame, complete with Robinson driving wheels and pony truck, the O1 was essentially a B1 - the boiler, cylinders, cab and Walschaerts valve gear all being new.

It was initially planned that one hundred and sixty of the O4's were to be converted to O1 standard and the first of these No.6595 appeared from Gorton works in February 1944 followed by another fifteen during that year. Another twenty-one O1's came out from Gorton in 1945 and thirteen more in 1946. Only one rebuild was carried out in 1947, two in 1948 and the last five in 1949. The programme was brought to a halt in 1949 after BR reviewed the situation regarding the 2-8-0 goods engines as a whole; large numbers of the WD Austerity had been bought by the LNER during 1946 and 1947 and BR itself purchased further batches of the Riddles designed 2-8-0 to satisfy their current requirements. Besides BR also wanted to standardise with their own, as yet to be built designs which in the end did not feature a 2-8-0 type.

From 1948 self-cleaning smokeboxes were fitted to most of the class at various works visits after rebuilding and these are indicated within the tables. The others got them at rebuilding.

Initially Gorton shed had each of the O1's as they came out of the shops from rebuilding but they then usually went to Colwick before returning to Gorton. Other places where they were tried out included Heaton, March, New England, Thornton Junction and Tyne Dock. Eventually most of the class settled at Annesley however, a small number ended up on the North Eastern Region and these were allocated to Tyne Dock shed.

Those engines which went to Tyne Dock were in 1952 each fitted with two Westinghouse pumps for working the iron ore trains from Terminus Quay to the steel works at Consett. Also fitted to these engines was a vacuum ejector for the train braking, the Westinghouse pumps being used only to close and open the wagon doors, each system independent of the other.

Though most of the class could be found at Annesley in the early 1950's, March shed received twenty-five O1's, all from Annesley, in 1957. Another five of the Annesley based engines went to Colwick at the same time. To take their place Annesley got an equal number of BR 9F 2-10-0's though their were still twenty-odd O1's left at the shed to work the coal traffic in the area. The BR 9F's took over the workings to Woodford which had been the domain of the Annesley O1's since their arrival at the shed.

Though Gorton looked after the class from the beginning, it was not unknown for those engines based at Tyne Dock shed to visit Gateshead or Darlington shops for light repairs. When Gorton works was being run down for closure in the early 1960's, the Eastern Region O1's started to visit Doncaster shops for general and other repairs and even Darlington from early 1964 after Doncaster had ceased steam locomotive repairs.

Withdrawals started in October 1962 when five of the class were condemned and no fewer than twenty-three were condemned at Annesley shed on 17th November 1962, some only weeks after receiving general overhauls and boiler changes. Annesley shed was at that time within the boundaries of the London Midland Region and no doubt the authorities saw fit to condemn perfectly good locomotives on the grounds that they were no longer required due to the influx of diesel locomotives. Many of these condemned engines were sent to Crewe works for cutting up after languishing for months on the dump at Annesley.

By the end of 1963 March had sent its surviving O1's to the ex-GC shed at Staveley and when that shed closed in 1965 the ten remaining O1's went to Langwith Junction (7) and the ex-Midland shed at Barrow Hill, Staveley (3). In July 1965 the last eight were condemned and Class O1 became extinct, outlived by many of the O4's that they were supposedly to have replaced.

Though Doncaster, Gorton, Crewe and even Derby works scrapped a number of the O1's, most ended up in the hands of the private scrap metal merchants during 1964 and 1965 as the BR workshops could no longer cope with the ever growing numbers of withdrawn steam locomotives at that period.

A great many classes of steam locomotives were scrapped during the last ten years of the BR steam era without a hint of preservation and that is something of a tragedy. However, the Great Central Railway 2-8-0 is represented in the National Collection by O4/1 No.63601, one of the earliest GC examples which virtually remained unaltered to withdrawal. The engine was withdrawn from Frodingham shed in 1963 and after a somewhat long period in store at various sites awaiting restoration, the engine is now fully restored and operational on the Great Central Railway at Loughborough.

NUMERICAL INDEX OF LOCOMOTIVES IN THIS VOLUME AND VOLUME 24A

1946/7 No.	'1924' No.	Page No.	1946/7 No.	'1924' No.	Page No.	1946/7 No.	'1924' No.	Page No.	1946/7 No.	'1924' No.	Page No.
			3567	6220	54, 223	3624	5399	33	3680	6346	100
			3568	6221	54	3625	5271	14	3680	6184	37
			3569	6222	54	3625	5348	18	3681	6347	100
3500	5966	37	3570	6223	57	3626	5001	9	3682	6548	139
3501	5026	9	3571	6224	57, 195	3627	5005	9	3683	6549	142
3502	5069	10	3572	6225	57	3628	5008	9	3683	6186	37
3503	5093	10	3572	5966	37	3629	6554	144	3684	6345	100
3504	5331	14	3573	6226	57	3630	6555	144, 198	3684	6187	39
3505	5332	14	3574	6227	57	3631	6556	144	3685	6344	100
3506	5333	15, 198	3575	6228	58	3632	6557	144	3686	6495	113
3507	5334	15	3576	6229	58	3632	5349	18	3687	6324	93, 204
3508	5335	15	3577	6230	58	3633	6536	135	3688	6343	100
3509	5102	10	3577	5026	9	3634	6377	113	3689	6341	99, 204
3510	5133	10	3578	6231	58, 195	3634	5350	18	3690	6551	142
3511	5155	14	3579	6232	58, 195	3635	6537	135	3690	6188	39
3512	5346	15	3580	6233	59	3635	5351	18	3691	6342	99
3513	5347	15	3580	5069	10	3636	6376	113	3692	6339	99
3514	5348	18	3581	6234	59	3637	6558	144	3692	6189	39
3515	5349	18	3582	6235	59	3638	6375	113	3693	6340	99
3516	5350	18	3582	5093	10	3639	6559	145	3693	6190	39
3517	5351	18	3583	6236	59	3640	6560	145	3694	6349	103
3518	5352	21	3584	6237	59	3640	5352	21	3695	6496	115
3519	5353	21	3585	6238	61	3641	6561	145	3696	6323	93
3520	5354	21	3585	5331	14	3642	6538	135	3697	6338	99
3521	5355	21	3586	6239	61	3643	6373	112	3698	6322	93
3522	5400	33	3586	5332	14	3643	5353	21	3698	6191	42
3523	5402	34	3587	6240	61	3644	6543	138	3699	6337	96
3524	5403	34	3588	6241	61	3645	6366	109	3700	6497	115
3525	5404	34	3589	6242	61, 195	3646	6374	112, 203	3700	6192	42
3526	5405	34	3590	6243	63, 195	3647	6544	139	3701	6498	115
3527	5406	35	3591	6244	63, 195	3648	6372	112	3702	6321	93
3528	5407	35	3592	6245	63, 198	3649	6365	109	3703	6336	96
3529	5408	35, 204	3593	6246	63	3650	6545	139, 203	3704	6550	142
3530	6183	37	3594	6247	63	3651	6539	135	3705	6320	91
3531	6184	37	3594	5333	15, 198	3652	6371	112, 203	3706	6319	91
3532	6185	37	3595	6248	64	3653	6370	112	3707	6499	115
3533	6186	37	3596	6249	64, 198	3654	6369	112	3707	6193	42
3534	6187	39	3597	6250	64	3654	5355	21	3708	6318	91
3535	6188	39	3598	6251	68	3655	6364	108	3709	6552	142
3536	6189	39	3598	5334	15	3656	6363	108	3710	6335	96
3537	6190	39	3599	6252	68	3657	6546	139	3710	6194	42
3538	6191	42	3600	5375	23	3658	6368	109	3711	6317	91
3539	6192	42	3600	5335	15	3658	5400	33	3711	6195	43, 204
3540	6193	42	3601	5376	23	3659	6360	105	3712	6334	96, 209
3541	6194	42	3601	5102	10	3660	6547	139	3713	6553	142
3542	6195	43, 204	3602	5377	23	3660	5403	34	3714	6316	90
3543	6196	43	3603	5378	23	3661	6540	138	3715	6333	96
3544	6197	43	3604	5379	23	3662	6358	105	3716	6310	89
3545	6198	43	3605	5380	24	3663	6359	105, 203	3717	6314	90
3546	6199	43	3606	5381	24	3664	6541	138	3718	6313	90
3547	6200	46	3607	5382	24	3664	5404	34	3719	6315	90
3548	6201	46	3607	5133	10	3665	6357	105	3719	6198	43
3549	6202	46	3608	5383	24	3666	6542	138	3720	6311	89
3550	6203	46	3608	5155	14	3667	6367	109	3721	6331	95
3551	6204	46	3609	5384	27	3668	6361	108	3722	6312	90
3552	6205	48	3610	5385	27, 198	3669	6362	108	3722	6199	43
3553	6206	48	3611	5386	27	3669	5405	34	3723	6330	95
3554	6207	48	3612	5387	27	3670	6356	105, 203	3723	6200	46
3555	6208	48	3613	5388	27	3671	6355	104	3724	6329	94
3556	6209	50	3614	5389	28	3671	5406	35	3725	6328	94, 209
3557	6210	50	3615	5390	28	3672	6354	104	3726	6500	115
3558	6211	50	3616	5391	28	3673	6352	104	3727	6327	94
3559	6212	50	3617	5392	30	3674	6351	103	3727	6201	46
3560	6213	51, 216	3617	5347	15	3675	6353	104	3728	6308	89
3561	6214	51, 216	3618	5393	30	3676	6350	103, 204	3729	6309	89
3562	6215	51	3619	5394	30, 198	3677	6348	103	3730	6326	94
3563	6216	51, 222	3620	5395	30	3677	5407	35	3731	6307	87
3564	6217	51	3621	5396	30	3678	6332	95	3732	6501	116
3565	6218	51	3622	5397	33	3678	5408	35, 204	3733	6502	116
3566	6219	54	3623	5398	33	3679	6325	93	3734	6503	116

O4/3. **No.6608 receiving a minor repair inside the former H&B erecting shop at Springhead works in the 1930's. This former Ministry of Munitions engine spent all of its LNER career working in the former North Eastern area, most of that time based in Hull. In BR days, as No.63823 it ended up at Ardsley shed and was amongst the last to be rebuilt to Part 8.**

Numbers in italics were allocated but not carried.
Page numbers are as follows:
Vol 24A 1-126; Vol 24B 127-228

O4/6. **The next to be altered was No.5012, ex works on 6th August 1926, which got a 1922 Gorton built boiler. Note that it did not have top feed or protection for superheater elements and was fitted with Intensifore lubrication for the cylinders and valves. The brake standpipe had the LNER Load class 7 collar. No.5012 still had original style of footsteps.**

O4/6. **Pace of conversion from O5 stepped up from 29th October 1932 when No.5017 became O4. No.5019, ex works 5th August 1933, had a Gorton built boiler with Gresley anti-vacuum valves and a 1ft 9in. plantpot chimney was put on. Nos.5014, 5015, 5017, 5019 and 5022, which had double side window cab, retained that feature. Note footsteps altered to the later style of a double one only at outer end of the crosshead slide bars. Gorton.**

CLASS O 4 continued.

6535

N.B. Loco. 22167 8/1919.

M of M 2076.

REPAIRS:
Gor. 16/5—8/8/25.**G.**
Gor. 10/12/27—21/1/28.**G.**
Gor. 28/6—19/7/30.**G.**
Gor. 9—23/7/32.**G.**
Gor. 26/8—16/9/33.**G.**
Gor. 22/6—6/7/35.**G.**
Intensifore removed.
Gor. 15—29/1/38.**G.**
Chimney altered.
Gor. 11—25/5/40.**G.**
Gor. 14—24/4/43.**G.**
Gor. 29/7—5/8/44.**L.**
Gor. 24/11/45.
Rebuilt to Class O1.

BOILERS:
1491.
1151 19/7/30.
 487 23/7/32.
1239 16/9/33.
1966 6/7/35.
3315 29/1/38.
3232 25/5/40.
3330 24/4/43.

SHEDS:
Gorton 4/8/25.
Doncaster 14/8/25.
Grantham 6/2/33.
Doncaster 21/11/42.
Colwick 7/9/43.
Doncaster 23/1/44.
Mexborough 12/3/44.
Doncaster 27/8/44.

RENUMBERED:
6535 8/8/25.

6536

Nasmyth Wilson 1260 7/1918.

M of M 1717.

REPAIRS:
Gor. 11/7—24/10/25.**G.**
Gor. 28/1—3/3/28.**G.**

Gor. 11/1—1/2/30.**G.**
Gor. 19—31/12/31.**G.**
Gor. 28/10—11/11/33.**G.**
Gor. 18/1—8/2/36.**G.**
Fountain lub. to axles.
Gor. 23/10—6/11/37.**H.**
Gor. 24/2—16/3/40.**G.**
Str. 26/11/42—7/1/43.**G.**
Gor. 14—28/10/44.**G.**
Gor. 19/12/45—12/1/46.**L.**
Tender only.
Gor. 1/3—26/4/47.**G.**
Rebuilt to Part 8.
Gor. 29/1—19/2/49.**G.**
Gor. 28/7—18/8/51.**G.**
Gor. 30/8—1/9/51.**N/C.**
Gor. 17/4—12/5/54.**G.**
Gor. 11—19/5/54.**N/C.**
Gor. 31/5—2/6/54.**N/C.**
Gor. 22/6—3/8/57.**G.**
Gor. 17/6—19/8/61.**G.**

BOILERS:
 1037.
 1139 3/3/28.
 1330 1/2/30.
 1087 31/12/31.
 1017 11/11/33.
 1490 8/2/36.
 3213 6/11/37.
 3389 16/3/40.
 1874 7/1/43.
 3382 28/10/44.
 5096 *(new)* 26/4/47.
 5098 *(exO1 3786)* 19/2/49.
 28338 *(ex63613)* 18/8/51.
 28852 *(new)* 12/5/54.
 28368 *(ex63836)* 3/8/57.
 28385 *(ex63675)* 19/8/61.

SHEDS:
Gorton 20/10/25.
Woodford 5/11/25.
Staveley 7/5/44.
Annesley 12/10/47.
Gorton 2/4/50.
Ardsley 22/9/52.

RENUMBERED:
6536 24/10/25.
3633 17/11/46.
63633 19/2/49.

CONDEMNED: 8/8/62.
Into Gor. for cut up 10/62.

6537

Nasmyth Wilson 1262 8/1918.

M of M 1719.

REPAIRS:
Gor. 18/7—31/10/25.**G.**
Gor. 28/1—10/3/28.**G.**
Gor. 28/6—19/7/30.**G.**
Gor. 19—26/3/32.**G.**
Gor. 3—10/11/34.**G.**
Gor. 28/11—12/12/36.**G.**
Gor. 4—18/3/39.**G.**
Gor. 8—20/9/41.**G.**

BOILERS:
1057.
1692 19/7/30.
 931 26/3/32.
1016 10/11/34.
3267 12/12/36.
1201 18/3/39.
3444 20/9/41.

SHEDS:
Gorton 29/10/25.
Woodford 13/11/25.
Doncaster 25/9/28.
Woodford 29/11/28.
Langwith Jct. 27/9/30.

RENUMBERED:
6537 31/10/25.

WITHDRAWN: 19/9/41.
*Reno. 748 and sent to Mid. East
via Ellesmere Port, 17/10/41.*

6538

Nasmyth Wilson 1285 ?/1919.

M of M 1729.

REPAIRS:
Gor. 30/5—10/10/25.**G.**
Gor. 22/10—26/11/27.**G.**
Gor. 15/3—12/4/30.**G.**
Gor. 19/3—2/4/32.**G.**
Gor. 11—25/8/34.**G.**
Gor. 18/7—1/8/36.**G.**
Fountain lub. to axles.
Gor. 13—20/8/38.**G.**
Gor. 14/12/40—4/1/41.**G.**
Gor. 17/9—2/10/43.**G.**
Gor. 21/7—4/8/45.**G.**
Gor. 4—25/10/47.**G.**
Gor. 4—18/2/50.**G.**

Gor. 5—26/4/52.**G.**
Gor. 29/5—19/6/54.**G.**
Gor. 22—24/6/54.**N/C.**
Gor. 12/1—9/2/57.**G.**
Gor. 12/11/59. *Not repaired.*

BOILERS:
1034.
1837 26/11/27.
1131 2/4/32.
1247 25/8/34.
1176 1/8/36.
3341 20/8/38.
3316 4/1/41.
1212 2/10/43.
3258 4/8/45.
3339 *(ex3736)* 25/10/47.
3427 *(ex3754)* 18/2/50.
22262 26/4/52.
22255 19/6/54.
22178 9/2/57.

SHEDS:
Gorton 6/10/25.
Immingham 15/10/25.
Woodford 10/4/30.
Langwith Jct. 27/9/30.
Frodingham 12/3/39.

RENUMBERED:
6538 10/10/25.
3642 13/12/46.
63642 18/2/50.

CONDEMNED: 18/11/59.
Cut up at Gorton.

6539

Kitson 5192 3/1918.

M of M 1610.

REPAIRS:
Gor. 1/6—1/8/25.**G.**
Gor. 16/4—3/7/28.**G.**
Gor. 12/6—24/7/30.**G.**
Gor. 25/4—4/6/32.**G.**
Gor. 5/7—4/8/34.**G.**
Fountain lub. to axles.
Gor. 9/6—1/7/36.**G.**
Gor. 22/3—2/5/38.**G.**
Chimney altered.
Gor. 27/5—15/6/40.**G.**
Str. 1/11/42—9/1/43.**G.**
Gor. 28/3—19/5/45.**G.**
Gor. 14/10—7/12/46.**G.**
Rebuilt to Part 8.
Gor. 16/12/48—29/1/49.**G.**

(above) O4/6. When No.5022 was converted on 5th October 1935, it got an ROD boiler and was still without anti-vacuum valve. An attempt at cutting to a 13ft 0in. height by fitting a 1ft 5½in. chimney was nullified by the cab still being out of gauge. Note the battleaxe shaped balance weights on the coupled wheels. Five O4/6 engines had this type of wheel sets: Nos.5014, 5019, 5420 which were all withdrawn in 1941 and sent to the Middle East, and 5015 (63917), 5022 (63920) which kept them to withdrawal by BR in June and August 1962 respectively (*see* photo O4/6/12 page).

(left) O4/6. Unless already altered as O5 class, the 1935/6 rebuilds had Intensifore lubricator taken off and replaced by Wakefield mechanical type.

O4/6. Beginning with No.5015, ex works on 29th June 1935, the 1ft 5½in. shaped cast chimney was introduced giving 12ft 10¾in. from rail level but the cab height was still 13ft 1½in. Gorton.

O4/6. To give a wider sphere of operation in emergency, the cab was brought within the 13ft 0in. gauge, starting with No.5019, ex works on 27th May 1939. No.5422, out on 23rd January 1943, was the completion of this cab change, which involved a further alteration to the shape of the front windows. Instead of a level base and sloping top, they were now semi-circular at the top and bottom. Note axlebox lubrication has been augmented by a fountain sight-feed in the cab. March shed, 6th April 1946.

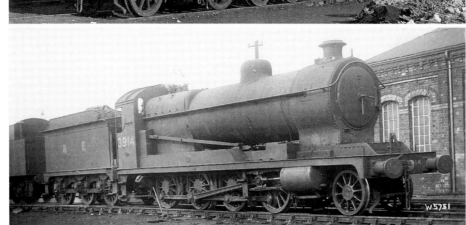

O4/6. From July 1942 only NE was put on the tender, and during 1946 the thirteen survivors were renumbered from 3902 to 3920. The six which were to have been Nos.3903, 3909, 3910, 3916, 3918, 3919 were sent to the War Department in 1941 and these numbers were not used. By the time No.5012 became 3914 on Sunday 13th October 1946, at Retford shed, its smokebox door wheel had been replaced by a second handle, and the tender had lost its water scoop.

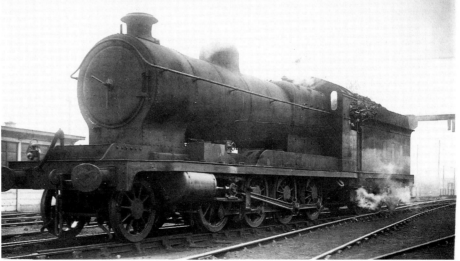

(right) O4/6. Starting with No.3917, ex works on 16th February 1946, LNER was restored, all except Nos.3904, 3916, 3913 and 3915, which went from NE to BRITISH RAILWAYS. No.3907 had LNER from 12th June 1946.

(below) O4/6. Of the thirteen engines no less than three got the E prefix to their number in 1948: E3904 (31st January), E3906 (21st February) and E3913 (18th February). Note that the upper lamp iron was still carried on top of the smokebox. A flat top dome cover was introduced during the 1939-45 war. Cambridge shed, March 1948.

6539 continued/.
Gor. 3/4—2/6/51.**G.**
Gor. 2—28/3/53.**G.**
Gor. 2/9—21/10/55.**G.**
Gor. 5/6—2/8/58.**G.**
Gor. 5/12/58—10/1/59.**C/L.**
Gor. 21/3—19/4/60.**C/L.**
Gor. 29/5—7/7/61.**H/I.**

BOILERS:
1296.
1124 24/7/30.
1837 4/6/32.
1075 4/8/34.
3248 1/7/36.
514 2/5/38.
3310 15/6/40.
3339 9/1/43.
3368 19/5/45.
5087 *(new)* 7/12/46.
5021 *(ex3613)* 29/1/49.
28321 *(exO1 63854)* 2/6/51.
28268 *(ex63853)* 28/3/53.
28885 *(new)* 21/10/55.
28881 *(ex63914)* 2/8/58.

SHEDS:
Gorton 1/8/25.
Colwick 18/8/25.
Langwith Jct. 16/9/27.
Immingham 18/12/49.
Colwick 23/9/62.
Retford 30/12/62.
Frodingham 13/6/65.

RENUMBERED:
6539 1/8/25.
3651 15/9/46.
63651 29/1/49.

CONDEMNED: 11/7/65.
Sold for scrap to Cox &
Danks, Wadsley Bridge, 8/65.

6540

Kitson 5208 7/1918.

M of M 1622.

REPAIRS:
Gor. ?/?—1/8/25.**G.**
Gor. ?/?—21/4/28.**G.**
Gor. 25/10—?/11/30.**G.**
Gor. 22—?/7/33.**G.**
Gor. 12—?/9/35.**G.**
Gor. 25/3—?/4/38.**G.**
Gor. 19/7—3/8/40.**G.**
Rebuilt to Part 7.
Gor. 27/8—10/10/42.**G.**
Gor. 12/3—7/4/44.**G.**
Gor. 29/7—28/9/46.**G.**
Gor. 7/11—11/12/48.**G.**
Gor. 6/1—2/2/52.**G.**

Gor. 5—7/2/52.**N/C.**
Gor. 18/5—19/6/54.**H.**
Gor. 16/2—23/3/57.**G.**
Gor. 24/7—14/9/61.**G.**

BOILERS:
1147.
1745 ?/11/30.
1140 ?/7/33.
1745 ?/9/35.
3324 ?/4/38.
3673 3/8/40.
3670 7/4/44.
3658 28/9/46.
5101 11/12/48.
22328 2/2/52.
22318 23/3/57.
22312 14/9/61.

SHEDS:
Gorton 1/8/25.
Colwick 18/8/25.
GWR. 23/11/40.
Woodford 30/7/42.
Darnall 3/2/46.
Staveley 27/3/60.
Mexborough 4/12/60.
Staveley 11/2/62.
Mexborough 9/9/62.
Darnall 9/12/62.
Mexborough 20/1/63.
Retford 22/9/63.
Frodingham 13/6/65.

RENUMBERED:
6540 1/8/25.
3661 10/1/47.
63661 11/12/48.

CONDEMNED: 8/8/65.
Sold for scrap to T.W. Ward,
Beighton, 9/65.

6541

Kitson 5212 8/1918.

M of M 1626.

REPAIRS:
Gor. 30/5—22/8/25.**G.**
Gor. 24/12/27—11/2/28.**G.**
Gor. 24/5—21/6/30.**G.**
Gor. 29/10—12/11/32.**G.**
Gor. 2—16/2/35.**G.**
Gor.1 —15/5/37.**G.**
Gor. 16—30/9/39.**G.**
Gor. 13—27/9/41.**G.**

BOILERS:
1206.
1417 21/6/30.
1493 12/11/32.
940 16/2/35.

1478 15/5/37.
3379 30/9/39.
820 27/9/41

SHEDS:
Gorton 20/8/25.
New England 2/9/25.
Colwick 19/10/32.

RENUMBERED:
6541 22/8/25.

WITHDRAWN: 19/9/41.
Reno.751 and sent to Mid. East.

6542

Kitson 5214 9/1918.

M of M 1628.

REPAIRS:
Gor. 18/7—24/10/25.**G.**
Gor. 3/12/27—21/1/28.**G.**
Gor. 25/4—16/5/31.**G.**
Gor. 7—28/7/34.**G.**
Gor. 24/7—7/8/37.**G.**
Fountain lub. to axles.
Gor. 15—22/6/40.**G.**
Gor. 26/6—10/7/43.**G.**
Gor. 1—22/12/45.**G.**
Gor. 24/4—15/5/48.**G.**
Gor. 9—23/6/51.**G.**
Gor. 8—18/7/51.**N/C.**
Gor. 28/8—25/9/54.**G.**
Gor. 26/4—31/5/58.**G.**

BOILERS:
1042.
1160 16/5/31.
1040 28/7/34.
1431 7/8/37.
3248 22/6/40.
1318 10/7/43.
3329 22/12/45.
3377 15/5/48.
22195 23/6/51.
22219 25/9/54.
22885 31/5/58.

SHEDS:
Gorton 22/10/25.
Woodford 5/11/25.
Neasden 18/12/28.
Mexborough 13/1/36.
Langwith Jct. 2/7/50.
Mexborough 10/9/50.
Immingham 22/9/52.
Mexborough 5/10/52.
Frodingham 27/12/59.

RENUMBERED:
6542 24/10/25.
3666 8/9/46.

63666 15/5/48.

CONDEMNED: 9/12/62.
Into Don. for cut up 27/8/63.

6543

Kitson 5185 1/1918.

M of M 1603.

To traffic 23/3/29.

REPAIRS:
Gor. 22/12/28—2/3/29.**G.**
Reb. to N.B. Load gauge & Pt 2.
Cow. 23/3—13/4/29.**L.**
Cow. 21/7—22/8/31.**G.**
Gor. 13/7—4/11/33.**G.**
Gor. 5—28/9/35.**G.**
Gor. 6/1—12/2/38.**G.**
Gor. 25/6—20/7/40.**G.**
Gor. 5/8—10/9/42.**G.**
Gor. 11/8—2/9/44.**G.**
Gor. 5/12/46—22/2/47.**G.**
Gor. 8/7—6/8/49.**G.**
Gor. 25—27/8/49.**N/C.**
Gor. 11/3—12/4/52.**G.**
Gor. 31/5—21/8/54.**G.**
Rebuilt to Part 8.
Gor. 28/1—9/3/57.**G.**
Gor. 8—15/11/58.**N/C.**
Gor. 23/11—22/12/59.**H/I.**
Gor. 16/11—28/12/62.**G.**

BOILERS:
518.
1443 4/11/33.
3211 28/9/35.
804 12/2/38.
1431 20/7/40.
3324 10/9/42.
1024 2/9/44.
945 22/2/47.
3344 6/8/49.
22260 12/4/52.
28338 *(ex63633)* 21/8/54.
28384 *(exO1 63854)* 9/3/57.
28378 *(ex63895)* 28/12/62.

SHEDS:
Thornton Jct. 23/3/29.
Mexborough 3/10/43.
Frodingham 16/9/45.
Doncaster 7/4/46.
Mexborough 8/9/46.
Langwith Jct. 5/9/47.
Tuxford 28/3/51.
Langwith Jct. 6/5/51.
Immingham 24/7/55.
Colwick 10/4/60.

6543 continued/.
RENUMBERED:
6543 2/3/29.
3644 24/11/46.
63644 6/8/49.

CONDEMNED: 15/1/66.
Sold for scrap to Geo. Cohen,
Kettering 3/66.

_____

6544

Kitson 5188 2/1918.

M of M 1606.

To traffic 19/12/28.

REPAIRS:
Gor. ?/?—13/10/28.**G**.
Rebuilt to N.B. Loading gauge
and Part 2 (LNE chimney).
Cow. 18/12/28.**L**.
Cow. 29/4—13/6/30.**G**.
Gor. 29/9—7/11/32.**G**.
Gor. 11/1—3/2/34.**G**.
Gor. 19/8—19/9/36.**G**.
Gor. 24—29/12/37.**N/C**.
Gor. 4/5—17/6/39.**G**.
Gor. 11/2—27/3/43.**G**.
Cow. 15—21/5/43.**L**.
Gor. 16/3—21/4/45.**G**.
Gor. 16/6—26/8/47.**G**.
Gor. 7/8—2/9/50.**G**.
Gor. 5/2—28/2/53.**G**.
Gor. 5/3—2/4/55.**G**.
Gor. 10/1—1/3/58.**G**.
Rebuilt to Part 8.
Gor. 12/10—19/11/59.**C/L**.
Gor. 18/3—27/4/61.**G**.

BOILERS:
1377.
C1470 7/11/32.
1042 3/2/34.
1188 19/9/36.
3262 27/3/43.
927 21/4/45.
3236 26/8/47.
22100 2/9/50.
22115 28/2/53.
22138 2/4/55.
28365 (exO1 63755) 1/3/58.
28973 (exO1 63670) 27/4/61.

SHEDS:
Dunfermline 19/12/28.
Langwith Jct. 27/7/43.
Doncaster 27/10/46.
Immingham 25/6/50.
Colwick 20/9/53.
Frodingham 21/6/59.
Retford 31/1/60.
Doncaster 3/3/63.

RENUMBERED:
6544 13/10/28.
3647 12/12/46.
63647 2/9/50.

CONDEMNED: 6/5/64.
Sold for scrap to Cox & Danks,
Wadsley Bridge, 6/64.

_____

6545

Kitson 5191 3/1918.

M of M 1609.

To traffic 3/5/29.

REPAIRS:
Gor. 26/1—4/5/29.**G**.
Gor. 1—22/8/31.**G**.
Gor. 18/11—2/12/33.**G**.
Gor. 18/4—2/5/36.**G**.
Fountain lub. to axles.
Gor. 25/6—9/7/38.**G**.
Gor. 21/12/40—4/1/41.**G**.
Gor. 19/5—6/6/42.**L**.
Gor. 3—20/2/43.**G**.
Gor. 3/3/45.
Rebuilt to Class O1.

BOILERS:
1338.
1227 22/8/31.
1046 2/12/33.
1318 2/5/36.
1881 9/7/38.
1002 4/1/41.
3244 20/2/43.

SHEDS:
Colwick 3/5/29.
Doncaster 23/1/44.

RENUMBERED:
6545 4/5/29.

_____

6546

Kitson 5204 6/1918.

M of M 1618.

To traffic 27/6/27.

REPAIRS:
Gor. 2/4—25/6/27.**G**.
Gor. 13/7—17/8/29.**G**.
Gor. 27/6—18/7/31.**G**.
Gor. 19/5—2/6/34.**G**.
Gor. 30/5—20/6/36.**G**.
Fountain lub. to axles.
Gor. 4—18/6/38.**G**.
Gor. 17—24/8/40.**G**.

Gor. 16/1—6/2/43.**G**.
Gor. 9—30/6/45.**G**.
Gor. 22/11—20/12/47.**G**.
Gor. 2—16/12/50.**G**.
Gor. 20—24/12/50.**N/C**.
Gor. 4—5/1/51.**N/C**.
Gor. 14—28/2/53.**G**.
Gor. 3—9/3/53.**N/C**.
Gor. 13/8—24/9/55.**G**.
Gor. 3/5—7/6/58.**G**.
Gor. 10—17/6/58.**N/C**.
Gor. 3—5/7/58.**N/C**.
Gor. 9—16/4/60.**N/C**.
Water Treatment fitted.

BOILERS:
1101.
930 18/7/31.
1112 2/6/34.
1122 20/6/36.
3227 18/6/38.
864 24/8/40.
3412 6/2/43.
1133 30/6/45.
3360 20/12/47.
22142 16/12/50.
22135 28/2/53.
22120 24/9/55.
22213 7/6/58.

SHEDS:
Doncaster 27/6/27.
Colwick 5/9/43.
Doncaster 23/1/44.
Mexborough 18/8/46.
Doncaster 20/10/47.
Immingham 25/6/50.
Colwick 20/9/53.

RENUMBERED:
6546 25/6/27.
3657 12/1/47.
63657 16/12/50.

CONDEMNED: 23/9/62.
Sold for scrap to Round Oak
Steel, Brierley Hill, 4/64.

_____

6547

Kitson 5207 7/1918.

M of M 1621.

To traffic 7/10/27.

REPAIRS:
Gor. 16/7—8/10/27.**G**.
Gor. 25/2—17/3/28.**L**.
Gor. 15/2—22/3/30.**G**.
Gor. 14—28/5/32.**G**.
Gor. 8—22/6/35.**G**.
Gor. 3—17/7/37.**G**.
Gor. 22/7—5/8/39.**G**.

Gor. 8—20/9/41.**G**.

BOILERS:
1212.
1173 28/5/32.
C1467 22/6/35.
857 17/7/37.
3286 5/8/39.
3442 20/9/41.

SHEDS:
Doncaster 7/10/27.
Retford 7/4/33.

RENUMBERED:
6547 8/10/27.

WITHDRAWN: 5/10/41.
Reno.738 and sent to Middle
East via Bidston, 14/10/41.

_____

6548

R. Stephenson 3708 12/1917.

M of M 1664.

To traffic 3/11/28.

REPAIRS:
Gor. 21/4—4/8/28.**G**.
Reb. to N.B. Load gauge & Pt 2.
Gor. 1—2/11/28.**N/C**.
Dunfermline shed. 4/2/29.
Side doors fitted.
Cow. 18/9—25/10/30.**G**.
Gor. 11—18/2/33.**G**.
Cow. 10—14/7/33.**L**.
Gor. 29/2—14/3/36.**G**.
Cow. 6/5—1/7/36.**L**.
Gor. 28/10—4/11/39.**G**.
Gor. 16—25/4/42.**G**.
Gor. 17/6—1/7/44.**G**.
Gor. 30/11—21/12/46.**G**.
Gor. 4—25/6/49.**G**.
Gor. 19/4—10/5/52.**G**.
Gor. 13—16/5/52.**N/C**.
Gor. 2—30/4/55.**G**.
Gor. 2/3/59. Not repaired.

BOILERS:
1937.
1942 18/2/33.
1069 14/3/36.
1090 4/11/39.
3205 25/4/42.
807 1/7/44.
1280 21/12/46.
3385 25/6/49.
22269 10/5/52.
22290 30/4/55.

SHEDS:
Dunfermline 3/11/28.

O4/6. Only three, Nos.63905, 63908 and 63911 did not have this style as they went from LNER to BR emblem. 63914 got the lettering ex works on 2nd April 1949 and had the lamp iron moved on to the smokebox door. Doncaster shed.

O4/6. Nos.63917 and 63920 retained the side window cab also the battleaxe balace weights, the other three with side window cabs having gone to the Middle East. From 24th September 1949, on 63905, the larger size BR emblem became standard. Frodingham shed, 16th August 1959.

(above) O4/6. **No.63902 ex works on 12th February 1955 had the 28in. size emblem and there was a further small detail change - from usual loose coupling to screw adjustable type. Langwith Junction shed, 19th February 1955.**

(right) O4/6. When 63902 was next out from a heavy repair - on 1st June 1957, it could have been expected to have the BR crest, but the change was only to the smaller 15½in. emblem. March, 29th March 1959.

O4/6. Apparently stock of the small emblem was being used up on goods engines because **63908, ex works on 1st March 1958 from general repair, still had it applied.** Mexborough, 15th June 1958.

6548 continued/.
Mexborough 6/10/43.
Frodingham 16/9/45.
Doncaster 7/4/46.
Mexborough 27/8/50.
Langwith Jct. 10/9/50.
Gorton 11/3/51.
Darnall 8/4/51.

RENUMBERED:
6548 4/8/28.
3682 21/12/46.
63682 25/6/49.

CONDEMNED: 6/3/59.
Cut up at Gorton.

6549

R. Stephenson 3709 1/1918.

M of M 1665.

To traffic 30/3/29.

REPAIRS:
Gor. 15/12/28—30/3/29.**G.**
Dar. 30/6—28/8/31.**G.**
Gor. 17/2—3/3/34.**G.**
Gor. 5—19/10/35.**G.**
Gor. 24/12/38—14/1/39.**G.**
Gor. 16—30/8/41.**G.**

BOILERS:
1462.
1864 3/3/34.
3215 19/10/35.
3234 14/1/39.
1075 30/8/41.

SHEDS:
York 30/3/29.
Hull Springhead 6/2/30.
Cudworth 7/2/30.
West Hartlepool 14/6/40.

RENUMBERED:
6549 30/3/29.

WITHDRAWN: 20/9/41.
*Reno.700 and sent to Middle
East via Birkenhead, 11/9/41.*

6550

R. Stephenson 3731 10/1918.

M of M 1647.

To traffic 2/12/28.

REPAIRS:
Gor. 28/7—10/11/28.**G.**

Reb. to N.B. Load gauge & Pt 2.
Cow. 3—11/12/28.**L.**
Thornton shed. 1/1/29.
Side doors fitted.
Cow. 15/4—16/5/31.**G.**
Gor. 18/4—20/5/33.**G.**
Gor. 20/4—11/5/35.**G.**
Gor. 27/3—17/4/37.**G.**
Gor. 6—20/5/39.**G.**
Gor. 16—26/7/41.**G.**
Gor. 27/8—11/9/43.**G.**
Gor. 19/4—2/6/47.**G.**
Gor. 18/10—10/11/50.**G.**
Gor. 24/10—5/12/53.**G.**
Rebuilt to Part 8.
Gor. 8—16/12/53.**N/C.**
Gor. 6/7—10/8/57.**G.**
Gor. 12/8—28/9/61.**H/I.**
Gor. 10—17/3/62.**C/L.**

BOILERS:
1418.
C1472 20/5/33.
1377 11/5/35.
3289 17/4/37.
3370 20/5/39.
3265 26/7/41.
3240 11/9/43.
3294 2/6/47.
22129 10/11/50.
28846 *(new)* 5/12/53.
28323 *(ex63750)* 10/8/57.

SHEDS:
Thornton Jct. 2/12/28.
Langwith Jct. 12/9/43.
March 8/9/44.
Cambridge 22/12/47.
March 29/3/48.
Mexborough 28/10/51.
Barnsley 13/2/55.
Langwith Jct. 29/11/59.
Mexborough 1/5/60.
Retford 9/7/61.

RENUMBERED:
6550 10/11/28.
3704 29/9/46.
63704 11/11/50.

CONDEMNED: 17/3/63.
Into Don. for cut up 19/8/63.

6551

R. Stephenson 3716 3/1918.

M of M 1672.

To traffic 1/12/28.

REPAIRS:
Gor. 14/7—1/12/28.**G.**
Reb. to N.B. Load gauge & Pt 2.

Cow. ?/?—21/11/31.**G.**
Gor. 10—17/12/32.**G.**
Gor. 25/3—1/4/33.**L.**
Gor. 4—11/5/35.**G.**
Gor. 27/3—17/4/37.**G.**
Gor. 27/5—17/6/39.**G.**
Gor. 8—20/9/41.**G.**

BOILERS:
1942.
C1467 17/12/32.
1271 11/5/35.
3287 17/4/37.
1016 17/6/39.
3441 20/9/41.

SHED:
Dundee 1/12/28.

RENUMBERED:
6551 1/12/28.

WITHDRAWN: 20/9/41.
*Reno.741 and sent to Middle
East via Bidston, 15/10/41.*

6552

R. Stephenson 3737 12/1918.

M of M 1689.

To traffic 12/8/27.

REPAIRS:
Gor. 7/5—13/8/27.**G.**
Gor. 21/9—26/10/29.**G.**
Gor. 4/7—1/8/31.**G.**
Gor. 11—25/11/33.**G.**
Gor. 9—23/5/36.**G.**
Fountain lub. to axles.
Gor. 2—16/7/38.**G.**
Gor. 28/9—5/10/40.**G.**
Gor. 1—8/5/43.**G.**
Gor. 22/9—6/10/45.**G.**
Gor. 22/3—5/4/47.**L.**
After collision.
Gor. 13/12/47—3/1/48.**G.**
Gor. 29/7—12/8/50.**G.**
Gor. 19—20/8/50.**N/C.**
Gor. 15/11—6/12/52.**G.**
Gor. 9—12/6/54.**C/L.**
Gor. 5/2—12/3/55.**G.**
Gor. 2/4/55.**C/L.**
After collision.
Gor. 18/1—22/2/58.**G.**
Rebuilt to Part 8.
Gor. 18/2/61. *Not repaired.*

BOILERS:
1146.
1962 1/8/31.
1167 25/11/33.
1182 23/5/36.

1864 16/7/38.
3231 5/10/40.
1029 8/5/43.
3269 6/10/45.
3258 3/1/48.
3396 12/8/50.
22879 6/12/52.
22279 12/3/55.
28946 *(new)* 22/2/58.

SHEDS:
Doncaster 12/8/27.
Mexborough 25/7/43.
Langwith Jct. 2/7/50.
Gorton 20/9/53.

RENUMBERED:
6552 13/8/27.
3709 15/8/46.
63709 12/8/50.

CONDEMNED: 23/2/61.
Cut up at Gorton.

6553

R. Stephenson 3741 1/1919.

M of M 1693.

To traffic 14/11/27.

REPAIRS:
Gor. 20/8—12/11/27.**G.**
Gor. 8/2—15/3/30.**G.**
Gor. 29/10—5/11/32.**G.**
Gor. 9—16/2/35.**G.**
Gor. 6—20/2/37.**G.**
Gor. 14—28/10/39.**G.**
Gor. 24/8—5/9/42.**G.**
Gor. 17/6—1/7/44.**G.**
Gor. 2—23/3/46.**G.**
Gor. 14—28/2/48.**G.**
Gor. 8/10/49.**C/L.**
Tender only.
Gor. 26/11—17/12/49.**G.**
Gor. 19/4—10/5/52.**G.**
Gor. 26/6—7/8/54.**G.**
Gor. 28/1—11/2/56.**C/L.**
Gor. 20/10—17/11/56.**G.**
Gor. 2/4—18/6/60.**H/I.**

BOILERS:
1216.
1178 5/11/32.
1250 16/2/35.
1181 20/2/37.
1280 28/10/39.
811 5/9/42.
3347 1/7/44.
856 23/3/46.
3405 28/2/48.
3213 17/12/49.
22267 10/5/52.

(above) O4/6. **Part 6 not only used up emblems but also tenders. 63907, on 12th October 1963, was coupled with tender 6017 which it had from 12th June 1946 to its 22nd May 1964 withdrawal. This tender was built in October 1901 and originally had open coal rails. By August 1935, they had been plated on the outside as proved by the absence of beading around the edge. Although 63907 had a heavy repair in March 1960 it shows no evidence of getting the BR crest. Mexborough shed, 12th October 1963.**

(right) O4/6. **Although 63912 did not get a smokebox number plate until out on 5th March 1949, it had been cast with the LNER version of the Gill sans 6 and 9 which was not a true one. Langwith Junction shed, 19th April 1963.**

O4/6. **British Railways withdrawal of Part 6 began with 63905 on 8th April 1959 but was only completed by that of 63913 on 6th June 1965 as shown here at Staveley shed on 19th June 1965, awaiting despatch to contractors for cutting up. Note electrification warning flash added above side footstep. Two Part 6 engines had been rebuilt by BR to Part 8, Nos.63914 in July 1955 and 63915 in January 1956.**

6553 continued/.
22259 7/8/54.
22203 17/11/56.

SHEDS:
Woodford 14/11/27.
Doncaster 24/9/28.
Mexborough 22/10/28.
Woodford 16/11/28.
Langwith Jct. 3/8/43.
Colwick 27/10/46.
Annesley 11/4/48.
Colwick 30/1/49.
Annesley 5/2/50.
Gorton 2/7/50.

RENUMBERED:
6553 12/11/27.
3713 23/3/46.
ᴇ**3713** 28/2/48.
63713 8/10/49.

CONDEMNED: 10/8/62.
Into Gor. for cut up 11/8/62.

_____

6554

Nasmyth Wilson 1244 12/1917.

M of M 1701.

To traffic 23/6/27.

REPAIRS:
Gor. 26/3—25/6/27.**G.**
Gor. 28/9—26/10/29.**G.**
Gor. 14—28/11/31.**G.**
Gor. 2—16/6/34.**G.**
Gor. 16—30/5/36.**G.**
Fountain lub. to axles.
Gor. 14—28/5/38.**G.**
Gor. 9—16/11/40.**G.**
Gor. 12—23/1/43.**G.**
Gor. 12/5—9/6/45.**G.**
Gor. 28/6—2/8/47.**G.**
Gor. 12—19/11/49.**G.**
Gor. 28/6—26/7/52.**G.**
Gor. 23/4—28/5/55.**G.**

BOILERS:
1090.
1951 28/11/31.
929 16/6/34.
3238 30/5/36.
3221 28/5/38.
3412 16/11/40.
3424 23/1/43.
1130 9/6/45.
3240 2/8/47.
1245 19/11/49.
22278 26/7/52.
22275 28/5/55.

SHEDS:
Doncaster 23/6/27.
Mexborough 25/7/43.
Darnall 1/7/45.

RENUMBERED:
6554 25/6/27.
3629 5/10/46.
63629 19/11/49.

CONDEMNED: 10/2/59.
Into Gor. for cut up 14/2/59.

_____

6555

Nasmyth Wilson 1255 2/1918.

M of M 1712.

To traffic 10/5/27.

REPAIRS:
Gor. 19/2—7/5/27.**G.**
Gor. 13/7—10/8/29.**G.**
Gor. 6—27/6/31.**G.**
Gor. 11—25/11/33.**G.**
Gor. 30/11—7/12/35.**G.**
Gor. 29/1—5/2/38.**G.**
Chimney altered.
Gor. 4—11/5/40.**G.**
Str. 23/9—31/10/42.**G.**
Gor. 21/4/45.
Rebuilt to Class O1.

BOILERS:
1009.
1468 27/6/31.
1366 25/11/33.
3222 7/12/35.
3216 5/2/38.
3329 11/5/40.
1019 31/10/42.

SHEDS:
Doncaster 10/5/27.
Mexborough 20/6/43.

RENUMBERED:
6555 7/5/27.

_____

6556

Nasmyth Wilson 1256 6/1918.

M of M 1713.

To traffic 3/7/28.

REPAIRS:
Gor. 28/4—7/7/28.**G.**
Gor. 31/5—5/7/30.**G.**
Gor. 1—8/10/32.**G.**
Gor. 22/12/34—5/1/35.**G.**

Gor. 6—13/3/37.**G.**
Gor. 8—22/4/39.**G.**
Gor. 25/6—12/7/41.**G.**
Gor. 11—23/10/43.**G.**
Gor. 8/2—8/3/47.**G.**
Gor. 1—31/7/48.**L.**
Gor. 6—13/11/48.**L.**
Tender only.
Gor. 13—27/8/49.**G.**
Gor. 29/12/51—19/1/52.**G.**
Gor. 5/6—3/7/54.**G.**
Gor. 24/11/56—5/1/57.**G.**
Rebuilt to Part 8.
Gor. 16/11—12/12/59.**H/I.**

BOILERS:
1277.
1056 8/10/32.
1219 5/1/35.
1266 13/3/37.
3265 22/4/39.
 853 12/7/41.
3317 23/10/43.
3230 8/3/47.
3223 27/8/49.
22237 19/1/52.
22240 3/7/54.
28925 *(new)* 5/1/57.

SHEDS:
Doncaster 3/7/28.
Gorton 7/2/43.
Colwick 22/4/45.
Annesley 12/10/47.
Colwick 1/2/48.
Annesley 4/12/49.
Gorton 16/7/50.

RENUMBERED:
6556 7/7/28.
3631 22/11/46.
63631 31/7/48.

CONDEMNED: 11/9/62.
Into Gor. for cut up 11/62.

_____

6557

Nasmyth Wilson 1259 7/1918.

M of M 1716.

To traffic 8/5/28.

REPAIRS:
Gor. 10/3—5/5/28.**G.**
Gor. 7/6—12/7/30.**G.**
Gor. 9—16/7/32.**G.**
Gor. 20—27/10/34.**G.**
Gor. 3—10/4/37.**G.**
Gor. 10—24/6/39.**G.**
Gor. 20/8—6/9/41.**G.**

BOILERS:
1319.
1249 16/7/32.
1359 27/10/34.
3285 10/4/37.
1228 24/6/39.
3433 6/9/41.

SHED:
Doncaster 8/5/28.

RENUMBERED:
6557 5/5/28.

WITHDRAWN: 13/9/41.
Reno.702 and sent to Middle
East via Birkenhead, 12/9/41.

_____

6558

Nasmyth Wilson 1265 10/1918.

M of M 1722.

To traffic 3/5/28.

REPAIRS:
Gor. 10/3—28/4/28.**G.**
Gor. 22/3—3/5/30.**G.**
Gor. 5—12/3/32.**G.**
Gor. 21/9—5/10/35.**G.**
Gor. 9—30/4/38.**G.**
Gor. 9—23/11/40.**G.**
Gor. 12/2—6/3/43.**G.**
Gor. 7—28/4/45.**G.**
Gor. 7/6—5/7/47.**G.**
Gor. 25/6—30/7/49.**G.**
Gor. 8—29/12/51.**G.**
Gor. 31/12/51—4/1/52.**N/C.**
Gor. 22/5—12/6/54.**L/I.**
Gor. 15—18/6/54.**N/C.**
Gor. 15/12/56—12/1/57.**G.**
Gor. 20—25/1/57.**N/C.**
Gor. 2/4—21/5/60.**H/I.**
Gor. 11—18/6/60.**N/C.**

BOILERS:
1315.
 853 12/3/32.
3212 5/10/35.
1237 30/4/38.
3298 23/11/40.
1130 6/3/43.
3381 28/4/45.
3223 5/7/47.
3224 30/7/49.
22234 29/12/51.
22202 12/1/57.

SHEDS:
Doncaster 3/5/28.
Immingham 19/9/33.
Retford 11/1/39.

6558 continued/.
RENUMBERED:
 6558 28/4/28.
 3637 16/11/46.
 63637 30/7/49.

CONDEMNED: 9/12/62.
Into Don. for cut up 16/9/63.

6559

Nasmyth Wilson 1267 10/1918.

M of M 1724.

To traffic 18/4/29.

REPAIRS:
Gor. 2/3—18/4/29.**G.**
Gor. 23/12/30—3/3/31.**G.**
Gor. 14/9—21/10/33.**G.**
Gor. 27/10—1/12/34.**G.**
Gor. 23/7—13/8/37.**G.**
Gor. 12—29/6/40.**G.**
Gor. 11/4—15/5/43.**G.**
Gor. 21/6—1/9/45.**G.**
Gor. 23/10—27/11/47.**G.**
Gor. 18/7—20/8/49.**G.**
Gor. 22/11—8/12/50.**C/H.**
Gor. 20—29/12/50.**N/C.**
Gor. 5/4—3/5/52.**G.**
Gor. 6—7/5/52.**N/C.**
Gor. 14—24/5/52.**N/C.**
Gor. 12/10—11/12/54.**G.**
Rebuilt to Part 8.
Gor. 5/9—12/10/57.**G.**
Gor. 17/3—20/4/60.**C/H.**
Gor. 23/7—29/8/62.**H/I.**
Gor. 3—7/9/62.**N/C.**

BOILERS:
 1246.
 1967 3/3/31.
 1478 21/10/33.
 933 1/12/34.
 3302 13/8/37.
 1940 29/6/40.
 1968 15/5/43.
 3410 1/9/45.
 3216 27/11/47.
 3296 20/8/49.
 22143 8/12/50.
 22266 3/5/52.
 28313 *(ex63828)* 11/12/54.
 28936 *(new)* 12/10/57.
 28825 *(ex63819)* 20/4/60.

SHEDS:
Doncaster 18/4/29.
Mexborough 1/5/29.
Colwick 28/1/45.
Annesley 30/5/48.
Colwick 28/9/52.
Annesley 22/1/56.

Colwick 17/6/56.

RENUMBERED:
 6559 18/4/29.
 3639 18/1/47.
 63639 20/8/49.

CONDEMNED: 19/12/65.
Sold for scrap to J. Cashmore,
Great Bridge, 2/66.

6560

Nasmyth Wilson 1283 9/1919.

M of M 1727.

To traffic 10/4/28.

REPAIRS:
Gor. 28/1—7/4/28.**G.**
Gor. 10/5—14/6/30.**G.**
Gor. 14—21/1/33.**G.**
Gor. 22/6—6/7/35.**G.**
Gor. 17/7—7/8/37.**G.**
Gor. 16—23/9/39.**G.**
Gor. 24/7—2/8/41.**G.**

BOILERS:
 863.
 1946 21/1/33.
 1058 6/7/35.
 1493 7/8/37.
 3378 23/9/39.
 3363 2/8/41.

SHEDS:
Mexborough 10/4/28.
Annesley 23/2/29.

RENUMBERED:
 6560 7/4/28.

WITHDRAWN: 13/9/41.
Reno.708 and sent to Middle
East via Glasgow, 16/9/41.

6561

Nasmyth Wilson 1284 9/1919.

M of M 1728.

To traffic 31/8/27.

REPAIRS:
Gor. 28/5—3/9/27.**G.**
Gor. 18/1—22/2/30.**G.**
Gor. 19—31/12/31.**G.**
Gor. 10—24/3/34.**G.**
Spring gear altered for working
to Whitemoor.
Gor. 20/6—4/7/36.**G.**

Fountain lub. to axles.
Gor. 27/8—24/9/38.**G.**
Gor. 30/11—7/12/40.**G.**
Gor. 1—26/6/43.**G.**
Gor. 21/4—19/5/45.**G.**
Gor. 23/4—18/5/46.**L.**
Gor. 18/10—15/11/47.**G.**
Gor. 3—17/12/49.**G.**
Gor. 20—26/12/49.**N/C.**
Gor. 16—23/9/50.**C/L.**
Gor. 13—18/11/50.**N/C.**
Gor. 10—24/5/52.**G.**
Gor. 27—30/5/52.**N/C.**
Gor. 25/9—16/10/54.**G.**
Gor. 10—12/11/55.**N/C.**
Gor. 27/4—1/6/57.**G.**
Rebuilt to Part 8.
Gor. 30/1—5/3/60.**H/I.**

BOILERS:
 1171.
 820 31/12/31.
 1462 24/3/34.
 1130 4/7/36.
 3343 24/9/38.
 3221 7/12/40.
 868 26/6/43.
 949 19/5/45.
 3425 15/11/47.
 1122 17/12/49.
 1122 reno.22111 23/9/50.
 22272 24/5/52.
 22221 16/10/54.
 28830 *(ex63653)* 1/6/57.

SHEDS:
New England 31/8/27.
Doncaster 24/2/30.
Frodingham 13/9/39.
Colwick 24/12/44.
Annesley 23/5/48.
Gorton 16/7/50.

RENUMBERED:
 6561 3/9/27.
 3641 15/1/47.
 63641 17/12/49.

CONDEMNED: 11/9/62.
Into Gor. for cut up 11/62.

6562

N.B. Loco. 21772 9/1917.

M of M 1805.

To traffic 25/10/27.

REPAIRS:
Gor. 23/7—22/10/27.**G.**
Gor. 15/3—12/4/30.**G.**
Gor. 26/3—9/4/32.**G.**
Gor. 15—29/6/35.**G.**

Gor. 21/8—4/9/37.**G.**
Gor. 27/1—10/2/40.**G.**
Gor. 30/7—14/8/43.**G.**
Gor. 10—24/3/45.**G.**
Gor. 30/11/46—11/1/47.**G.**
Gor. 11—24/12/48.**G.**
Gor. 3—24/3/51.**G.**
Gor. 28/3—2/4/51.**N/C.**
Gor. 23/5—13/6/53.**G.**
Gor. 16—22/6/53.**N/C.**
Gor. 3/9—1/10/55.**G.**
Gor. 11/8—1/9/56.**C/L.**
Gor. 11—27/1/57.**C/L.**
Gor. 29/1—1/2/57.**N/C.**
Gor. 5/3—2/4/60.**G.**

BOILERS:
 1241.
 1058 9/4/32.
 1297 29/6/35.
 1867 4/9/37.
 1432 10/2/40.
 3254 14/8/43.
 3380 24/3/45.
 1115 11/1/47.
 3217 24/12/48.
 22169 24/3/51.
 22175 13/6/53.
 22118 1/10/55.
 22890 2/4/60.

SHEDS:
Doncaster 25/10/27.
Immingham 22/9/33.
GWR. 23/11/40.
Woodford 21/1/43.
Gorton 10/3/43.
Annesley 1/4/45.
Woodford 29/6/47.
Annesley 12/10/47.
Colwick 11/9/49.
March 9/3/52.
Colwick 30/3/52.
Staveley 27/12/53.

RENUMBERED:
 6562 22/1/27.
 3735 1/9/46.
 63735 24/12/48.

CONDEMNED: 29/12/62.
Into Don. for cut up 20/9/63.

6563

N.B. Loco. 21773 9/1917.

M of M 1806.

To traffic 17/2/28.

REPAIRS:
Gor. 5/11/27—18/2/28.**G.**
Gor. 15/3—12/4/30.**G.**

O4/7. **The fourteen engines rebuilt from Part 1 to Part 7 retained their steam brake on the engine and tender, with vacuum ejector for train brakes and were the only Part 7 so fitted. All Part 7 cab roofs had flat strips for strengthening instead of angle iron used hitherto. Mexborough shed, 18th April 1947.**

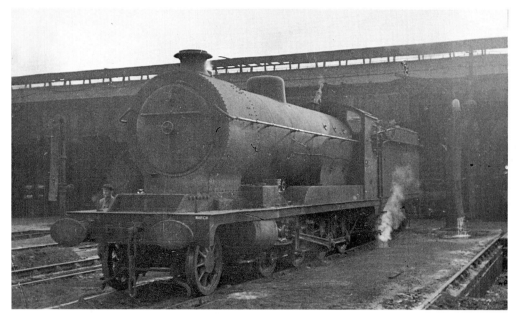

O4/7. **Nos.6286 and 6352 from Part 2 lost their cut-down cab which they had needed in Scottish Area, but both kept the tenders with the high front plate which Cowlairs had put on in November 1931 and January 1932. They lost these tenders later, in October 1949 and May 1946 respectively. Stratford shed, 13th October 1945.**

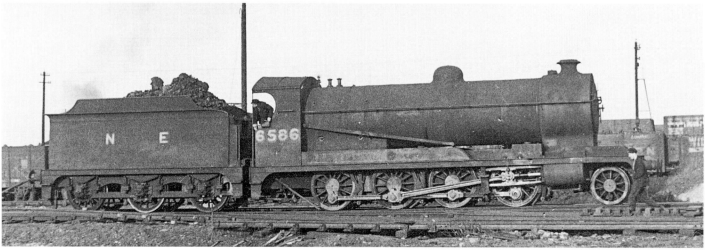

O4/7. **Part 3 contributed twenty-four to Part 7 and three, Nos.6300, 6612 and 6633 actually exchanged ROD built boilers for the 5ft 6in. diameter. March shed, 6th April 1946.**

O4/7. **This conversion 3½ years after rebuilding to Part 7 had apparently ceased, from Part 5, occurred because Diagram 15A boilers were reaching the end of their useful life, and six spare 15D boilers had been built, so one could be used to advantage. No.3705 kept its outside fillers to the rear sandboxes; all other Part 7 had them in the cab. Gorton, 30th May 1950.**

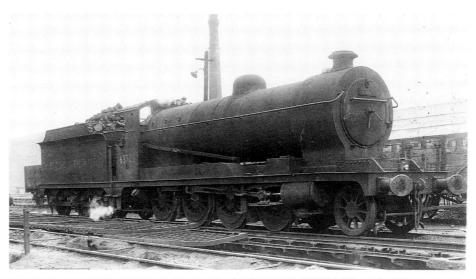

O4/7. **The larger diameter boiler pushed the reversing rod nearer to the cab side and a 'blister' had to be put on the panel to enable the handle to turn full circle.**

O4/7. **Until 1946/7, the smokebox door continued to have a wheel and handle fastening. No.3860, ex works on 22nd November 1947, was unusual in retaining a wheel.**

6563 continued/.
Gor. 19/12/31—9/1/32.**G.**
Gor. 3—17/8/35.**G.**
Gor. 24/7—7/8/37.**G.**
Gor. 7—21/10/39.**G.**
Gor. 30/9—11/10/41.**G.**

BOILERS:
1272.
1001 9/1/32.
3205 17/8/35.
3301 7/8/37.
3346 11/10/41.

SHEDS:
Doncaster 17/2/28.
Immingham 22/9/33.

RENUMBERED:
6563 18/2/28.

WITHDRAWN: 18/10/41.
Reno.783 and sent to Mid East.

6564

N.B. Loco. 21774 9/1917.

M of M 1807.

To traffic 2/9/27.

REPAIRS:
Gor. 4/6—3/9/27.**G.**
Gor. 21/9—26/10/29.**G.**
Gor. 6—27/6/31.**G.**
Gor. 9—16/12/33.**G.**
Gor. 30/11—14/12/35.**G.**
Gor. 19—26/2/38.**G.**
Fountain lub. to axles.
Gor. 1—8/6/40.**G.**
Gor. 9—20/3/43.**G.**
Gor. 10/11—8/12/45.**G.**
Gor. 15/11—6/12/47.**G.**
Gor. 25/3—15/4/50.**G.**
Gor. 2—23/8/52.**G.**
Gor. 19/12/53—9/1/54.**C/L.**
Gor. 10—19/1/54.**N/C.**
Gor. 14/5—25/6/55.**G.**
Gor. 2—4/7/55.**N/C.**
Gor. 16—20/8/58.**G.**
Gor. 13—16/10/58.**N/C.**
Gor. 12/9—10/10/59.**C/L.**

BOILERS:
1175.
1961 27/6/31.
1227 16/12/33.
3223 14/12/35.
1003 26/2/38.
3398 8/6/40.
3313 20/3/43.
3318 8/12/45.
3275 6/12/47.

3425 15/4/50.
22287 23/8/52.
22143 25/6/55.
22146 20/8/58.

SHEDS:
Doncaster 2/9/27.
Mexborough 25/7/43.
Darnall 27/4/47.

RENUMBERED:
6564 3/9/27.
3737 11/8/46.
63737 15/4/50.

CONDEMNED: 9/12/62.
Into Horwich for cut up 6/63.

6565

N.B. Loco. 21776 9/1917.

M of M 1809.

To traffic 19/12/27.

REPAIRS:
Gor. 3/9—17/12/27.**G.**
Gor. 8/3—5/4/30.**G.**
Gor. 17—24/9/32.**G.**
Gor. 5—12/1/35.**G.**
Gor. 3—17/4/37.**G.**
Gor. 29/7—12/8/39.**G.**
Gor. 6—23/8/41.**G.**

BOILERS:
1223.
1210 24/9/32.
858 12/1/35.
3288 17/4/37.
857 12/8/39.
3322 23/8/41.

SHEDS:
New England 19/12/27.
Colwick 29/8/32.

RENUMBERED:
6565 17/12/27.

WITHDRAWN: 9/9/41.
Reno.709 and sent to Middle East via Glasgow 16/9/41.

6566

N.B. Loco. 21779 10/1917.

M of M 1812.

To Traffic 19/5/27.

REPAIRS:
Gor. 5/3—21/5/27.**G.**
Gor. 1/6—13/7/29.**G.**
Gor. 6—20/6/31.**G.**
Gor. 22—29/7/33.**G.**
Gor. 16—23/11/35.**G.**
Gor. 11—24/12/37.**G.**
Gor. 6—13/7/40.**G.**
Gor. 5—20/3/43.**G.**
Gor. 5/5/45.
Rebuilt to Class O1.

BOILERS:
1017.
1808 20/6/31.
1234 29/7/33.
1038 23/11/35.
1089 24/12/37.
1021 13/7/40.
3302 20/3/43.

SHEDS:
Doncaster 19/5/27.
GWR. 21/11/40.
Woodford 29/1/43.
West Hartlepool 20/3/43.
Hull Dairycoates 5/3/45.

RENUMBERED:
6566 21/5/27.

6567

N.B. Loco. 21782 10/1917.

M of M 1815.

To traffic 25/10/28.

REPAIRS:
Gor. ?/?—25/10/28.**G.**
Gor. 29/11/30—19/1/31.**G.**
Gor. 25/2—1/4/33.**G.**
Gor. 18/2—16/3/35.**G.**
Gor. 18/7—8/8/36.**G.**
Gor. 28/11/38—7/1/39.**G.**
Gor. 13/1—1/2/41.**G.**
Gor. 12—13/9/41.
Examined for W.D.
Gor. 11/3—17/4/43.**G.**
Gor. 11/11/45—5/1/46.**G.**
Gor. 4/1—13/2/48.**G.**
Gor. 18/10—5/11/49.**C/H.**
Gor. 9—11/11/49.**N/C.**
Gor. 2/11—2/12/50.**G.**
Gor. 6—9/12/50.**N/C.**
Gor. 22/11—13/12/52.**G.**
Gor. 27/4—4/6/55.**G.**
Gor. 16/5—5/7/58.**G.**
Rebuilt to Part 8.
Gor. 17/5—24/6/61.**H/I.**
Gor. 28/3—7/4/62.**N/C.**

BOILERS:
1431.
1027 19/1/31.
1314 1/4/33.
855 16/3/35.
1943 8/8/36.
1256 7/1/39.
3351 1/2/41.
3224 17/4/43.
3333 5/1/46.
1284 13/2/48.
22138 2/12/50.
22884 13/12/52.
22273 4/6/55.
28969 *(new)* 5/7/58.

SHEDS:
Gorton 25/10/28.
Mexborough 27/1/46.
Doncaster 18/8/46.
Langwith Jct. 25/6/50.
Frodingham 10/9/50.

RENUMBERED:
6567 25/10/28.
3741 18/8/46.
ᴇ3741 13/2/48.
63741 5/11/49.

CONDEMNED: 4/4/65.
Sold for scrap to J. Cashmore, Great Bridge, 5/65.

6568

N.B. Loco. 21783 10/1917.

M of M 1816.

To traffic 23/6/27.

REPAIRS:
Gor. 26/3—25/6/27.**G.**
Gor. 13/7—17/8/29.**G.**
Gor. 20—27/2/32.**G.**
Gor. 12—26/5/34.**G.**
Gor. 4—18/7/36.**G.**
Gor. 5—19/11/38.**G.**
Gor. 12/4—10/5/41.**G.**
Gor. 8—18/12/43.**G.**
Gor. 16/6—21/7/45.**L.**
Gor. 8/3—19/4/47.**G.**
Gor. 9—23/10/48.**H.**
Gor. 28/5—18/6/49.**G.**
Gor. 23/6—28/7/51.**G.**
Gor. 30/7—1/8/51.**N/C.**
Gorton 22/8—5/9/53.**G.**
Gor. 8—12/9/53.**N/C.**
Gor. 29/10—5/11/55.**C/L.**
Gor. 4/8—22/9/56.**G.**
Rebuilt to Part 8.
Gor. 23/11—14/12/57.**C/L.**
Gor. 17—20/12/57.**N/C.**
Gor. 27/8—24/9/60.**H/I.**

O4/7. When No.3749 was ex works on 25th May 1946, it had been changed from wheel to another handle on the smokebox door. Note the wide oval buffer heads and upper lamp iron with cloverleaf bracket in a more accessible position, on the door. Langwith Jct. shed, 4th August 1946.

O4/7. No.63634 was from Part 1 but the water scoop had been removed from the tender and no Part 7 was noted having pick-up apparatus. This was a December 1939 built boiler and so had normal rounded dome cover. The upper lamp iron is now Group Standard with more clearance from the door. Tuxford, May 1950.

6568 continued/.

BOILERS:
1080.
1265 27/2/32.
1191 26/5/34.
1868 18/7/36.
3355 19/11/38.
3253 10/5/41.
1237 18/12/43.
1287 18/6/49.
22201 28/7/51.
22204 5/9/53.
28921 (new) 22/9/56.

SHEDS:
Immingham 23/6/27.
Keadby 27/2/30.
Immingham 17/3/32.
Frodingham 11/6/32.
Colwick 12/9/44.
Annesley 12/10/47.
Gorton 20/10/50.
Darnall 13/6/54.

RENUMBERED:
6568 25/6/27.
3742 1/9/46.
63742 23/10/48.

CONDEMNED: 10/2/63.
Into Horwich for cut up 6/63.

_____

6569

N.B. Loco. 21784 10/1917.

M of M 1817.

to traffic 3/6/27.

REPAIRS:
Gor. 19/3—4/6/27.**G.**
Gor. 22/2—29/3/30.**G.**
Gor. 11—18/2/33.**G.**
Gor. 6—20/7/35.**G.**
Gor. 21/8—4/9/37.**G.**
Gor. 25/6—2/7/38.**L.**
After collision.
Gor. 27/1—10/2/40.**G.**
Gor. 4—9/8/41.**H.**
Gor. 10—20/9/41.**L.**

BOILERS:
1050.
1959 18/2/33.
C1473 20/7/35.
933 4/9/37.
3220 10/2/40.
1007 9/8/41.

SHEDS:
Immingham 3/6/27.
Keadby 7/1/31.
Frodingham 12/6/32.

RENUMBERED:
6569 4/6/27.

WITHDRAWN: 21/9/41.
Reno.742 and sent to Middle
East via Bidston 15/10/41.

_____

6570

N.B. Loco. 21787 10/1917.

M of M 1820.

To traffic 11/8/27.

REPAIRS:
Gor. 7/5—13/8/27.**G.**
Gor. 28/9—2/11/29.**G.**
Gor. 9—30/7/32.**G.**
Gor. 23/6—7/7/34.**G.**
Gor. 26/9—10/10/36.**G.**
Gor. 22—29/4/39.**G.**
Gor. 18—27/9/41.**G.**

BOILERS:
1144.
1331 30/7/32.
1190 7/7/34.
1146 10/10/36.
1266 29/4/39.
3268 27/9/41.

SHEDS:
Immingham 11/8/27.
Neasden 5/11/29.
Woodford 13/2/31.

RENUMBERED:
6570 13/8/27.

WITHDRAWN: 19/9/41.
Reno.760 and sent to Mid. East.

_____

6571

N.B. Loco. 21788 10/1917.

M of M 1821.

To traffic 25/7/27.

REPAIRS:
Gor. 23/4—23/7/27.**G.**
Gor. 26/10—30/11/29.**G.**
Gor. 25/1—1/2/30.**L.**
Gor. 23—30/4/32.**G.**
Gor. 14—28/7/34.**G.**
Fountain lub. to axles.
Gor. 22/8—5/9/36.**G.**
Gor. 24/9—15/10/38.**G.**
Gor. 22/2—15/3/41.**G.**
Gor. 21/1—14/2/42.**L.**
Gor. 12—27/11/42.**H.**

Gor. 2—23/11/46.**G.**
Gor. 31/1—14/2/48.**L.**
Gor. 11/9/48.
Rebuilt to Class O1.

BOILERS:
1132.
1315 30/4/32.
1206 28/7/34.
546 5/9/36.
1176 15/3/41.
3245 27/11/43.
3309 23/11/46.

SHEDS:
Immingham 25/7/27.
Frodingham 1/9/34.
Colwick 11/9/44.
Staveley 9/11/47.

RENUMBERED:
6571 23/7/27.
3746 1/9/46.
ᴇ**3746** 14/2/48.

_____

6572

N.B. Loco. 21791 11/1917.

M of M 1824.

To traffic 12/5/27.

REPAIRS:
Gor. 19/2—14/5/27.**G.**
Gor. 28/9—2/11/29.**G.**
Gor. 14/11—5/12/31.**G.**
Gor. 9—23/12/33.**G.**
Gor. 30/11—14/12/35.**G.**
Gor. 14—28/5/38.**G.**
Chimney altered.
Gor. 11—25/11/39.**G.**
Str. 13/6—18/7/42.**G.**
Rebuilt to Part 7.
Gor. 19/8—2/9/44.**G.**
Gor. 28/4—19/5/45.**L.**
Gor. 21/6—26/7/47.**G.**
Gor. 20/3—10/4/48.**H.**
Gor. 19/8—9/9/50.**G.**
Gor. 16—28/9/50.**N/C.**
Gor. 18/10—1/11/52.**G.**
Gor. 4—7/11/52.**N/C.**
Gor. 23/4—21/5/55.**G.**
Gor. 8—29/3/58.**G.**
Gor. 6/5/61. Not repaired..

BOILERS:
1015.
1864 5/12/31.
1949 23/12/33.
3224 14/12/35.
3206 28/5/38.
3683 18/7/42.
3684 2/9/44.

3660 26/7/47.
22300 9/9/50.
22301 1/11/52.
22310 21/5/55.
22873 29/3/58.

SHEDS:
Ardsley 12/5/27.
Immingham 10/9/27.
Keadby 27/2/30.
Frodingham 12/6/32.
Doncaster 7/4/46.
Mexborough 8/9/46.
Frodingham 25/12/49.

RENUMBERED:
6572 14/5/27.
3747 19/7/46.
63747 10/4/48.

CONDEMNED: 18/5/61.
Cut up at Gorton.

_____

6573

N.B. Loco. 21796 11/1917.

M of M 1829.

To traffic 24/4/28.

REPAIRS:
Gor. 4/2—14/4/28.**G.**
Gor. 28/3—18/4/31.**G.**
Gor. 21/10—4/11/33.**G.**
Gor. 3—17/8/35.**G.**
Gor. 13—27/11/37.**G.**
Gor. 27/4—18/5/40.**G.**
Rebuilt to Part 7.
Gor. 12—29/8/42.**G.**
Gor. 5—23/9/44.**G.**
Gor. 27/4—25/5/46.**G.**
Gor. 12—26/4/47.**L.**
Gor. 26/6—7/8/48.**G.**
Gor. 7—14/1/50.**C/L.**
Gor. 7—21/10/50.**G.**
Gor. 10—17/5/52.**C/H.**
Gor. 20—22/5/52.**N/C.**
Gor. 13/6—4/7/53.**G.**
Gor. 5/3—2/4/55.**C/H.**
Gor. 24/3—5/5/56.**C/H.**
Gor. 26/1—23/2/57.**G.**
Gor. 27/10/59. Not repaired.

BOILERS:
864.
1871 18/4/31.
1025 4/11/33.
3204 17/8/35.
1880 27/11/37.
3668 18/5/40.
3673 23/9/44.
3694 25/5/46.
3675 7/8/48.

6573 continued/.
22305 21/10/50.
22334 17/5/52.
22308 4/7/53.
22339 2/4/55.
22321 23/2/57.

SHEDS:
Colwick 24/4/28.
GWR. 28/11/40.
Woodford 23/7/42.
Langwith Jct. 3/8/43.
Colwick 27/10/46.
Staveley 9/11/47.

RENUMBERED:
  6573 14/4/28.
  3749 25/5/46.
63749 7/8/48.

CONDEMNED: 31/10/59.
Cut up at Gorton.

─────────────────────

6574

N.B. Loco. 21800 12/1917.

M of M 1833.

To traffic 16/9/27.

REPAIRS:
Gor. 4/6—17/9/27.**G**.
Gor. 30/11/29—11/1/30.**G**.
Gor. 13—20/8/32.**G**.
Gor. 9—23/3/35.**G**.
Gor. 26/6—10/7/37.**G**.
Gor. 23/9—7/10/39.**G**.
Gor. 3—22/8/42.**G**.
Gor. 14—28/10/44.**G**.
Gor. 21/9—12/10/46.**G**.
Gor. 15—22/11/47.**H**.
Gor. 15/1—5/2/49.**G**.
Gor. 10—31/5/52.**G**.
Gor. 19/2—17/3/55.**G**.
Gor. 19—20/3/55.**N/C**.
Gor. 23/2—2/3/57.**C/L**.
Gor. 5—7/3/57.**N/C**.
Gor. 9/3/59. *Not repaired.*

BOILERS:
  1185.
  1115 20/8/32.
  1944 23/3/35.
  3299 10/7/37.
  1362 7/10/39.
  3294 22/8/42.
  3392 *(ex6522)* 28/10/44.
  1020 12/10/46.
  1006 *(ex3697)* 5/2/49.
22196 31/5/52.
22891 17/3/55.

SHEDS:
Immingham 16/9/27.
Gorton 30/8/40.
York 11/9/40.
Heaton 28/3/43.
Tyne Dock 23/7/45.
Cudworth 7/11/48.
Royston 12/8/51.
Colwick 2/9/51.
Annesley 18/10/53.
Colwick 27/12/53.
Mexborough 29/1/56.

RENUMBERED:
  6574 17/9/27.
  3751 12/10/46.
63751 5/2/49.

CONDEMNED: 12/3/59.
Cut up at Gorton.

─────────────────────

6575

N.B. Loco. 21801 12/1917.

M of M 1834.

To traffic 19/4/27.

REPAIRS:
Gor. 12/2—9/4/27.**G**.
Gor. 6/7—3/8/29.**G**.
Gor. 27/6—18/7/31.**G**.
Gor. 16—30/9/33.**G**.
Gor. 13—20/7/35.**G**.
Gor. 14—28/8/37.**G**.
Gor. 9—16/12/39.**G**.
Gor. 19—28/2/42.**G**.
Gor. 5—29/4/45.**G**.
Gor. 25/8/45.
Rebuilt to Class O1.

BOILERS:
1003.
1054 18/7/31.
1120 30/9/33.
1945 20/7/35.
1040 28/8/37.
3214 16/12/39.
1115 28/2/42.
3269 29/4/45.

SHEDS:
Gorton 19/4/27.
Annesley 6/10/37.
Colwick 13/10/40.
Doncaster 23/1/44.
Ardsley 25/6/45.

RENUMBERED:
6575 9/4/27.

─────────────────────

6576

N.B. Loco. 21803 12/1917.

M of M 1836.

To traffic 21/4/28.

REPAIRS:
Gor. 25/2—21/4/28.**G**.
Dar. 4/10—29/11/30.**G**.
Gor. 15—29/4/33.**G**.
Gor. 12—26/5/34.**L**.
Gor. 25/5—8/6/35.**G**.
Gor. 19/6—3/7/37.**G**.
Gor. 8—22/4/39.**G**.
Gor. 29/3—12/4/41.**G**.
Gor. 24/2—13/3/43.**G**.
Gor. 19/5—16/6/45.**G**.
Gor. 11/10—1/11/47.**G**.
Gor. 25/2—11/3/50.**G**.
Gor. 13—27/9/52.**G**.
Gor. 1—2/10/52.**N/C**.
Gor. 8/10—12/11/55.**G**.
Gor. 23—26/11/55.**N/C**.
Gor. 25/5—1/6/57.**C/L**.
Gor. 28/11/59. *Not repaired.*

BOILERS:
  867.
  179 29/4/33.
  1263 8/6/35.
  1937 3/7/37.
  1869 22/4/39.
  3263 *(ex6513)* 12/4/41.
  1118 16/6/45.
  3386 *(ex3672)* 1/11/47.
  3317 11/3/50.
22296 27/9/52.
22104 12/11/55.

SHEDS:
York 21/4/28.
Tyne Dock 15/3/29.
York 13/5/29.
Cudworth 5/10/29.
Heaton 28/3/43.
Tyne Dock 23/7/45.
Heaton 22/7/46.
Tyne Dock 8/9/46.
Hull Dairycoates 6/2/49.
Hull Springhead 15/4/51.
Doncaster 2/9/51.
Mexborough 28/10/51.
Doncaster 21/11/54.
Mexborough 6/2/55.

RENUMBERED:
  6576 21/4/28.
  3753 8/9/46.
63753 11/3/50.

CONDEMNED: 2/12/59.
Cut up at Gorton.

─────────────────────

6577

N.B. Loco. 21806 12/1917.

M of M 1839.

To traffic 31/3/28.

REPAIRS:
Gor. ?/?—31/3/28.**G**.
Dar. 29/11/30—31/1/31.**G**.
Dar. 15/7—5/8/33.**G**.
Gor. 8/2—16/3/35.**G**.
Gor. 24/7—7/8/37.**G**.
Gor. 27/11—23/12/39.**G**.
Gor. 14/3—4/4/42.**G**.
Gor. 7/11—26/12/42.**L**.
Gor. 18/12/43—8/1/44.**G**.
Gor. 19/9—26/10/46.**G**.
Gor. 12/8—10/9/49.**G**.
Gor. 28/3—3/5/52.**G**.
Gor. 6—17/5/52.**N/C**.
Gor. 16/8—16/9/54.**G**.
Gor. 11/6—24/8/57.**G**.
Rebuilt to Part 8.
Gor. 17/9—30/10/57.**N/C**.
Gor. 23/3—22/4/60.**C/H**.
Gor. 16/1—16/2/62.**H/I**.

BOILERS:
  861.
  1307 31/1/31.
  938 5/8/33.
  1936 16/3/35.
  1005 7/8/37.
  3230 *(ex6195)* 4/4/42.
  1090 *(ex6614)* 8/1/44.
  3427 26/10/46.
  3422 *(ex3607)* 10/9/49.
22264 3/5/52.
22267 16/9/54.
28387 *(exO1 63578)* 24/8/57.
28386 *(exO1 63740)* 22/4/60.

SHEDS:
Hull Dairycoates 31/3/28.
Hull Springhead 18/11/29.
Cudworth 7/2/30.
Hull Springhead 8/1/40.
Heaton 24/2/40.
Tyne Dock 23/7/45.
Heaton 22/7/46.
Tyne Dock 8/9/46.
Hull Dairycoates 6/2/49.
Hull Springhead 4/12/49.
Hull Dairycoates 21/5/50.
Cudworth 12/11/50.
Royston 12/8/51.
Colwick 2/9/51.

RENUMBERED:
  6577 31/3/28.
  3754 26/10/46.
63754 10/9/49.

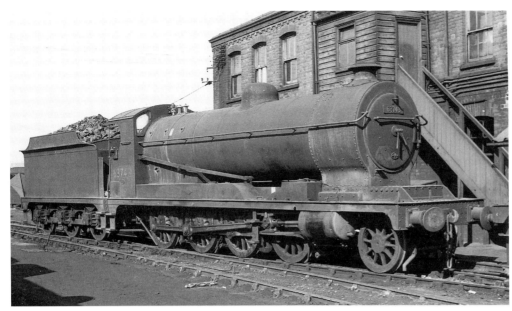

O4/7. **This boiler on 63748 to its 26th November 1962 withdrawal, kept the round top dome cover with which it had been fitted when built in March 1940. Doncaster shed, May 1961.**

O4/7. **The boilers built from November 1942 had a flat top to the dome cover, for ease of production, as reduced height was not a necessity. March shed, April 1946.**

O4/7. **Although those rebuilt from Part 1 retained train-braking facility, and some acquired screw coupling, no evidence has been found of a Part 7 engine working a passenger train.**

O4/7. **No.63848 (ex 6291) kept the tender with a high front plate to August 1956, this having been fitted by Cowlairs in November 1931. Gorton shed, 23rd March 1952.**

(above) O4/7. **No.63673 (ex 6352)** which got a high front to its tender at Cowlairs in January 1932, lost that tender in May 1946 and then had a low front type through to withdrawal.

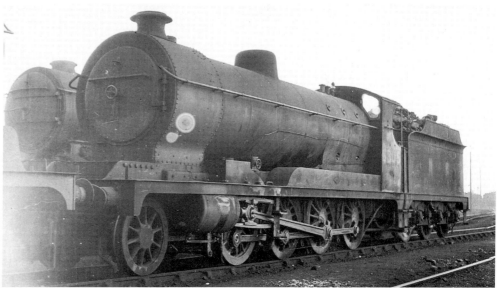

O4/7. **No.6305, to Part 7 on 4th March 1944, had only NE on its tender and from July 1942 to early 1946 all ran in that style.**

6577 continued/.
CONDEMNED: 7/2/64.
Sold for scrap to A.Looms,
Spondon, 4/64.

_____

6578

N.B. Loco. 21807 12/1917.

M of M 1840.

To traffic 21/1/28.

REPAIRS:
Gor. 31/12/27—21/1/28.**G**.
Dar. 28/4—29/7/30.**G**.
Gor. 22—29/4/33.**G**.
Gor. 18/5—1/6/35.**G**.
Gor. 25/9—9/10/37.**G**.
Gor. 15—29/6/40.**G**.
Gor. 28/9—10/10/42.**G**.
Gor. 19/8/44.
Rebuilt to Class O1.

BOILERS:
1308.
1945 29/4/33.
1302 1/6/35.
1200 9/10/37.
1271 29/6/40.
3319 10/10/42.

SHEDS:
Hull Dairycoates 21/1/28.
Hull Springhead 18/11/29.
Cudworth 7/2/30.
Hull Springhead 8/1/40.
West Hartlepool 18/5/40.

RENUMBERED:
6578 21/1/28.

_____

6579

N.B. Loco. 21826 2/1918.

M of M 1849.

To traffic 12/5/28.

REPAIRS:
Gor. 3/3—12/5/28.**G**.
Dar. 23/1—5/3/31.**G**.
Gor. 11/3—1/4/33.**G**.
Gor. 15—22/12/34.**G**.
Gor. 15—22/8/36.**G**.
Gor. 19/11—3/12/38.**G**.
Gor. 1—15/3/41.**G**.
Gor. 16/11—4/12/43.**G**.

Gor. 10—17/2/45.**L**.
Gor. 25/5/46.
Rebuilt to Class O1.

BOILERS:
1318.
1876 5/3/31.
1948 1/4/33.
1142 22/12/34.
 486 22/8/36.
1863 3/12/38.
1150 15/3/41.
3337 4/12/43.

SHEDS:
York 12/5/28.
Hull Springhead 21/8/30.
Cudworth 12/1/34.
Heaton 28/3/43.
Tyne Dock 23/7/45.

RENUMBERED:
6579 12/5/28.

_____

6580

N.B. Loco. 21831 3/1918.

M of M 1854.

To traffic 19/5/28.

REPAIRS:
Gor. 17/3—19/5/28.**G**.
Dar. 29/9—14/11/30.**G**.
Gor. 24/6—1/7/33.**G**.
Gor. 9—23/11/35.**G**.
Gor. 23/4—14/5/38.**G**.
Gor. 11—25/1/41.**G**.

BOILERS:
 871.
1036 1/7/33.
1217 23/11/35.
1413 14/5/38.
3341 (ex6538) 25/1/41.

SHEDS:
York 19/5/28.
Hull Springhead 5/10/29.
Hull Dairycoates 11/7/33.
Cudworth 30/10/36.
Heaton 1/4/40.

RENUMBERED:
6580 19/5/28.

WITHDRAWN: 20/9/41.
Reno.765 and sent to Mid. East.

_____

6581

N.B. Loco. 21834 3/1918.

M of M 1857.

To traffic 26/5/28.

REPAIRS:
Gor. 12—26/5/28.**G**.
Dar. 8/4—5/7/30.**G**.
Gor. 5/8—3/10/33.**G**.
Gor. 17/8—14/9/35.**G**.
Gor. 3/4—1/5/37.**G**.
Gor. 4/6—2/7/38.**G**.
Gor. 2/12/39—6/1/40.**G**.
Gor. 28/3—18/4/42.**G**.
Gor. 27/5—24/6/44.**G**.
Gor. 7/2—9/3/46.**G**.
Gor. 3/5—12/6/48.**G**.
Gor. 14/9—8/10/49.**C/H**.
Gor. 16/6—9/8/50.**G**.
Gor. 16/10—15/11/52.**G**.
Gor. 10/1—19/2/55.**C/L**.
Gor. 21/12/55—4/2/56.**C/L**.
Gor. 7/2—8/3/58.**G**.
Gor. 8/2—17/3/62.**G**.

BOILERS:
1321.
1307 3/10/33.
1020 14/9/35.
1314 1/5/37.
 42 2/7/38.
949 6/1/40.
 855 (ex6344) 18/4/42.
1285 24/6/44.
3351 (ex6615) 9/3/46.
3329 (ex3666) 12/6/48.
3263 9/8/50.
22185 15/11/52.
22172 8/3/58.
22233 17/3/62.

SHEDS:
Hull Dairycoates 26/5/28.
Hull Springhead 27/9/29.
West Hartlepool 9/5/40.
Hull Springhead 13/1/45.
Hull Dairycoates 29/4/46.
Doncaster 2/9/51.
Mexborough 15/5/55.
Frodingham 27/12/59.
Retford 20/11/60.
Doncaster 3/3/63.

RENUMBERED:
6581 26/5/28.
3764 16/6/46.
63764 12/6/48.

CONDEMNED: 27/2/66.
Sold for scrap to T.W. Ward,
Beighton, 4/66.

_____

6582

N.B. Loco. 21836 3/1918.

M of M 1859.

To traffic 15/1/29.

REPAIRS:
Gor. 28/7—8/12/28.**G**.
Reb. to N.B. Load gauge & Pt 2.
Cow. 11—12/1/29.**N/C**.
Fitted with side doors.
Cow. 3—29/8/31.**G**.
Gor. 8—22/7/33.**G**.
Gor. 2—16/11/35.**G**.
Gor. 14/1—4/2/39.**G**.
Gor. 8—19/7/41.**G**.
Gor. 15—24/12/43.**G**.
Gor. 16/2—9/3/46.**G**.
Gor. 24/4—22/5/48.**G**.
Gor. 13—27/1/51.**G**.
Gor. 5—6/2/51.**N/C**.
Gor. 15/8—5/9/53.**G**.
Gor. 21/4—19/5/56.**G**.
Gor. 10/1—7/2/59.**G**.
Gor. 1/4/61.Weigh only.
Gor. 25/8/62. Not repaired.

BOILERS:
1443.
1038 22/7/33.
1187 16/11/35.
 655 4/2/39.
3279 19/7/41.
1176 24/12/43.
 815 9/3/46.
3331 22/5/48.
22156 27/1/51.
22189 5/9/53.
22165 19/5/56.
22138 7/2/59.

SHEDS:
Aberdeen Ferryhill 15/1/29.
Dundee ?/10/30.
Dunfermline 29/7/43.
Doncaster 30/9/43.
Darnall 25/6/45.
Colwick 21/6/53.
Gorton 21/11/54.

RENUMBERED:
6582 8/12/28.
3766 26/5/46.
63766 22/5/48.

_____

WORKS CODES:- Bpk - Beyer, Peacock. Crw - Crewe. Cw - Cowlairs. Dar- Darlington. Dby - Derby. Don - Doncaster. Ghd - Gateshead. Gor - Gorton. Inv - Inverurie. Str - Stratford.
REPAIR CODES:- **C/H** - Casual Heavy. **C/L** - Casual Light. **G** - General. **H**- Heavy. **H/I** - Heavy Intermediate. **L** - Light. **L/I** - Light Intermediate. **N/C** - Non-Classified.

6582 continued/.
CONDEMNED: 26/8/62.
Cut up at Gorton.

6583

N.B. Loco. 21839 4/1918.

M of M 1862.

To traffic 24/1/28.

REPAIRS:
Gor. 15/10/27—28/1/28.**G.**
Dar. 21/2—17/4/30.**G.**
Gor. 28/1—11/2/33.**G.**
Gor. 9—16/2/35.**G.**
Gor. 20/3—3/4/37.**G.**
Gor. 16—23/12/39.**G.**
Gor. 11—25/4/42.**G.**
Gor. 25/3—15/4/44.**G.**
Gor. 22/12/45—5/1/46.**L.**
Gor. 15/3—5/4/47.**G.**
Gor. 4/6—2/7/49.**G.**
Gor. 17/11—8/12/51.**G.**
Gor. 4/12/54—22/1/55.**H.**
Gor. 16/9—14/12/57.**C/L.**
Gor. 24/12/57—8/1/58.**N/C.**
Gor. 25/2/59. *Not repaired.*

BOILERS:
1264.
  859 11/2/33.
  822 16/2/35.
3281 3/4/37.
1955 23/12/39.
1081 *(ex5400)* 25/4/42.
3306 *(ex6370)* 15/4/44
3245 *(ex3746)* 5/4/47.
1941 2/7/49.
22231 8/12/51.

SHEDS:
Doncaster 24/1/28.
Hull Dairycoates 28/1/28.
Hull Springhead 24/3/30.
Heaton 24/2/40.
Tyne Dock 23/7/45.
Hull Dairycoates 6/2/49.
Doncaster 2/9/51.

RENUMBERED:
6583 28/1/28.
3769 8/9/46.
63769 2/7/49.

CONDEMNED: 6/3/59.
Cut up at Gorton.

6584

N.B. Loco. 21840 4/1918.

M of M 1863.

To traffic 24/3/28.

REPAIRS:
Gor. 17—24/3/28.**G.**
Dar. 15/11—31/12/30.**G.**
Gor. 26/8—21/10/33.**G.**
Gor. 30/11—30/12/35.**G.**
Gor. 2/4—7/5/38.**G.**
Gor. 16/5—15/6/40.**G.**
Rebuilt to Part 7.
Dar. 1/1/42. Weigh.
Gor. 7/11—12/12/42.**G.**
Gor. 18/9—9/10/43.**L.**
Gor. 9/1—3/3/45.**G.**
Gor. 21/6—9/8/47.**G.**
Gor. 14/9—22/10/49.**G.**
Gor. 17/5—14/6/52.**G.**
Gor. 27/8—1/10/53.**C/L.**
Gor. 16/2—25/3/55.**G.**
Gor. 1/5—16/6/56.**C/L.**
Gor. 17/10—16/11/57.**G.**
Gor. 10/2—18/3/61.**G.**
Gor. 25/3—6/4/61.**N/C.**
Gor. 19—29/4/61.**N/C.**

BOILERS:
1307.
  868 31/12/30.
  487 21/10/33.
1458 30/12/35.
3248 7/5/38.
3672 15/6/40.
3667 *(ex6319)* 3/3/45.
3679 *(ex6300)* 9/8/47.
3674 *(ex3775)* 22/10/49.
22335 14/6/52.
22314 25/3/55.
22309 16/11/57.
22302 18/3/61.

SHEDS:
Hull Dairycoates 24/3/28.
Hull Springhead 18/11/29.
West Hartlepool 10/5/41.
Hull Dairycoates 5/3/45.
Hull Springhead 15/4/51.
WR. (Southall) 2/9/51.
Immingham 16/9/51.
Colwick 7/12/58.

RENUMBERED:
6584 24/3/28.
3770 16/6/46.
63770 22/10/49.

CONDEMNED: 19/12/65.
Sold for scrap to J.Cashmore,
Great Bridge, 2/66.

6585

N.B. Loco. 21843 4/1918.

M of M 1866.

To traffic 22/10/27.

REPAIRS:
Gor. 23/7—22/10/27.**G.**
Gor. 5/10—9/11/29.**G.**
Gor. 25/6—9/7/32.**G.**
Gor. 5—19/1/35.**G.**
Gor. 24/4—8/5/37.**G.**
Gor. 22—29/7/39.**G.**
Gor. 16—27/9/41.**G.**

BOILERS:
1203.
1043 9/7/32.
1692 19/1/35.
  859 8/5/37
1065 29/7/39.
3220 27/9/41.

SHED:
Langwith Jct. 22/10/27.

RENUMBERED:
6585 22/10/27.

WITHDRAWN: 19/9/41.
Reno.758 and sent to Mid. East.

6586

N.B. Loco. 21846 4/1918.

M of M 1869.

To traffic 31/12/27.

REPAIRS:
Gor. 1/10—31/12/27.**G.**
Gor. 2/8—6/9/30.**G.**
Gor. 27/5—17/6/33.**G.**
Gor. 7—14/12/35.**G.**
Gor. 11/6—2/7/38.**G.**
Gor. 3—24/8/40.**G.**
Rebuilt to Part 7.
Gor. 19/2—14/3/42.**G.**
Gor. 17—24/6/44.**G.**
Gor. 19/10—2/11/46.**G.**
Gor. 7—21/5/49.**G.**
Gor. 1—15/12/51.**G.**
Gor. 21/5—25/6/55.**G.**
Gor. 17/1—14/2/59.**G.**

BOILERS:
1244.
1036 6/9/30.
1003 17/6/33.
3226 14/12/35.
3335 2/7/38.

3674 24/8/40.
3664 14/3/42.
3685 24/6/44.
3674 2/11/46.
3678 21/5/49.
22326 15/12/51.
22338 25/6/55.
22301 14/2/59.

SHEDS:
Colwick 31/12/27.
GWR. 22/11/40.
Woodford 24/7/42.
Colwick 4/9/42.
Doncaster 23/1/44.
Gorton 25/6/45.
Mexborough 8/7/45.
Retford 16/12/45.
Mexborough 27/8/50.
Gorton 20/1/57.

RENUMBERED:
6586 31/12/27.
3775 2/11/46.
63775 21/5/49.

CONDEMNED: 22/3/62.
Into Gor. for cut up 24/3/62.

6587

N.B. Loco. 21851 5/1918.

M of M 1874.

To traffic 7/11/27.

REPAIRS:
Gor. 20/8—5/11/27.**G.**
Gor. 25/1—22/2/30.**G.**
Gor. 25/6—9/7/32.**G.**
Gor. 28/7—4/8/34.**G.**
Gor. 5—19/12/36.**G.**
Gor. 22/7—19/8/39.**G.**
Gor. 8—13/9/41.**G.**

BOILERS:
1217.
1331 22/2/30.
1132 9/7/32.
1201 4/8/34.
3270 19/12/36.
3419 13/9/41.

SHEDS:
New England 7/11/27.
Colwick 9/8/32.

RENUMBERED:
6587 5/11/27.

WITHDRAWN: 14/9/41.
Reno.728 and sent to Middle
East via Glasgow, 8/10/41.

6588

N.B. Loco. 21852 5/1918.

M of M 1875.

To traffic 5/7/27.

REPAIRS:
Gor. 2/4—25/6/27.**G.**
Gor. 17/8—21/9/29.**G.**
Gor. 5—26/9/31.**G.**
Gor. 20—27/1/34.**G.**
Gor. 8—22/2/36.**G.**
Fountain lub. to axles.
Gor. 16—30/4/38.**G.**
Gor. 9—23/3/40.**G.**
Gor. 26/10—2/11/40.**H.**
Str. 1/5—29/6/42.**G.**
Gor. 5—26/6/43.**G.**
Gor. 19/5—9/6/45.**G.**
Gor. 15/11—6/12/47.**G.**
Gor. 10—31/12/49.**G.**
Gor. 9—10/1/50.**N/C.**
Gor. 13—27/9/52.**G.**
Gor. 1—2/10/52.**N/C.**
Gor. 31/3—28/4/56.**G.**
Gor. 25/10—15/11/58.**C/H.**

BOILERS:
1112.
1101 26/9/31.
1883 27/1/34.
1002 22/2/36.
3235 30/4/38.
3242 23/3/40.
3233 2/11/40.
3258 29/6/42.
3324 9/6/45.
3325 6/12/47.
3395 31/12/49.
22297 27/9/52.
22283 28/4/56.

SHEDS:
Langwith Jct. 5/7/27.

March 25/11/36.
Cambridge 22/12/47.
Mexborough 11/1/50.
Retford 16/7/61.

RENUMBERED:
6588 25/6/27.
3779 29/9/46.
63779 31/12/49.

CONDEMNED: 13/4/62.
Into Gor. for cut up 14/4/62.

_____

6589

N.B. Loco. 21857 5/1918.

M of M 1880.

To traffic 16/2/28.

REPAIRS:
Gor. 19/11/27—18/2/28.**G.**
Gor. 28/12/29—25/1/30.**G.**
Gor. 14—28/5/32.**G.**
Gor. 19—26/1/35.**G.**
Gor. 15—29/5/37.**G.**
Gor. 11—25/11/39.**G.**
Gor. 9—16/5/42.**G.**
Gor. 21/2—4/3/44.**G.**
Gor. 24/8—14/9/46.**G.**
Gor. 20/11—11/12/48.**G.**
Gor. 13/10—3/11/51.**G.**
Gor. 6—10/11/51.**N/C.**
Gor. 4/9—2/10/54.**G.**
Gor. 6—15/10/54.**N/C.**
Gor. 9/11—7/12/57.**C/L.**
Gor. 11—14/12/57.**N/C.**
Gor. 6/9—4/10/58.**G.**
Gor. 13—17/10/58.**N/C.**
Gor. 24—28/10/58.**N/C.**

BOILERS:
1936.
1082 28/5/32.

1056 26/1/35.
822 29/5/37.
1104 16/5/42.
3277 4/3/44.
3201 14/9/46.
1950 11/12/48.
22221 3/11/51.
22282 2/10/54.
22258 4/10/58.

SHEDS:
Sheffield 16/2/28.
Retford 24/2/34.
Sheffield 4/11/35.
Staveley 29/7/38.
Woodford 11/8/44.
Darnall 3/2/46.
Colwick 6/3/49.
Darnall 7/8/49.

RENUMBERED:
6589 18/2/28.
3783 26/5/46.
63783 11/12/48.

CONDEMNED: 9/12/62.
Into Dby. for cut up 7/63.

_____

6590

N.B. Loco. 21859 5/1918.

M of M 1882.

To traffic 6/1/28.

REPAIRS:
Gor. 12/11/27—6/1/28.**G.**
Gor. 5/5—16/7/29.**G.**
Gor. 26/10—5/12/31.**G.**
Gor. 29/1—3/3/34.**G.**
Gor. 12/3—11/4/36.**G.**
Fountain lub. to axles.
Gor. 6/8—5/10/38.**G.**
Gor. 17/9—12/10/40.**G.**

Gor. 6/9—3/10/42.**G.**
Gor. 22/9—4/11/44.**G.**
Rebuilt to Part 8.
Gor. 18/6—17/8/46.**G.**
Gor. 9/1—19/2/49.**G.**
Gor. 10—24/3/49.**N/C.**
Gor. 25/4—26/5/51.**G.**
Gor. 31/5—1/6/51.**N/C.**
Gor. 1—29/8/53.**G.**
Gor. 1/4—1/5/54.**C/L.**
Gor. 10/4—12/5/56.**G.**
Gor. 15/1—16/2/59.**G.**
Gor. 31/3—14/5/60.**C/L.**
Gor. 7/5—22/6/62.**H/I.**

BOILERS:
825.
1034 5/12/31.
1875 3/3/34.
1050 11/4/36.
1130 5/10/38.
1135 12/10/40.
3385 3/10/42.
5027 *(new)* 4/11/44.
5007 *(exO1 3867)* 17/8/46.
5028 *(ex3853)* 19/2/49.
28317 *(exB1 61156)* 26/5/51.
28321 *(ex63651)* 29/8/53.
28895 *(new)* 12/5/56.
28880 *(ex63624)* 16/2/59.

SHEDS:
New England 6/1/28.
Sheffield 16/7/29.
Retford 20/3/34.
Doncaster 13/6/65.

RENUMBERED:
6590 6/1/28.
3785 17/8/46.
63785 19/2/49.

CONDEMNED: 27/3/66.
Sold for scrap to T.W. Ward,
Beighton, 5/66.

_____

O4/7. **LNER was restored from January 1946 and until the end of December 1947 Gorton managed to find shaded transfers for it and for the figures. Much of the renumbering was first done at the shed, using 6in. stencils (*see* page 146, top), and No.6358 became 3662 in that style on Sunday 8th December 1946 at Colwick shed. It got these shaded transfers ex works on 8th March 1947. Doncaster shed, 17th May 1947.**

O4/7. Six Part 7 got the BR prefix E in 1948: E3570 (7th February), E3600 (17th January), E3616 (6th March), E3772 (13th March), E3824 (24th January), E3843 (24th January). As No.E3570 got a general repair, Gorton were clearly reluctant to change from LNER. Tuxford, 4th April 1948.

O4/7. No.63891 got this style ex works on 13th August 1948 including true Gill sans 6 and 9 on the cab, although the smokebox number plate was cast with the modified version.

O4/7. From September 1949 the lettering was replaced by the emblem and the larger (28in.) size was standard.

O4/7. The emblem was handed for the lion to face forward on both sides, which was permissible when the emblem had no heraldic status.

6591

N.B. Loco. 21862 6/1918.

M of M 1885.

To traffic 14/8/28.

REPAIRS:
Gor. 12/5—11/8/28.**G.**
Gor. 25/1—8/2/30.**G.**
Gor. 5—19/12/31.**G.**
Gor. 9—23/6/34.**G.**
Gor. 1—15/8/36.**G.**
Fountain lub. to axles.
Gor. 22/10—5/11/38.**G.**
Gor. 7—21/12/40.**G.**
Gor. 6—15/8/42.**G.**
Gor. 30/12/43—22/1/44.**G.**
Gor. 31/8—21/9/46.**G.**
Gor. 4—11/10/47.**H.**
Gor. 29/1—12/2/49.**G.**
Gor. 28/4—19/5/51.**G.**
Gor. 21—23/5/51.**N/C.**
Gor. 26/9—10/10/53.**G.**
Gor. 13—17/10/53.**N/C.**
Gor. 14/1—4/2/56.**C/H.**
Gor. 16/1—6/4/57.**L/I.**
Gor. 9—20/4/57.**N/C.**
Gor. 3—22/5/57.**N/C.**
Gor. 27/2—2/4/60.**C/L.**
Gor. 5/6/62. *Not repaired.*

BOILERS:
1749.
1153 8/2/30.
803 19/12/31.
1330 23/6/34.
1215 15/8/36.
3258 5/11/38.
1350 21/12/40.
3277 15/8/42.
1882 22/1/44.
3345 21/9/46.
3256 12/2/49.
22186 19/5/51.
22201 10/10/53.
22210 4/2/56.

SHEDS:
Doncaster 14/8/28.
Langwith Jct. 14/5/43.
Colwick 19/9/44.
Annesley 18/12/49.
Colwick 8/1/50.
Annesley 8/10/50.
Gorton 26/11/50.
Staveley 4/5/52.

RENUMBERED:
6591 11/8/28.

3787 21/9/46.
63787 12/2/49.

CONDEMNED: 8/6/62.
Cut up at Gorton.

6592

N.B. Loco. 21863 6/1918.

M of M 1886.

To traffic 30/9/27.

REPAIRS:
Gor. 20/8—1/10/27.**G.**
Gor. 12/10—9/12/29.**G.**
Gor. 6/6—15/7/32.**G.**
Gor. 30/1—23/2/35.**G.**
Gor. 23/6—24/7/37.**G.**
Gor. 25/7—17/9/39.**G.**
Rebuilt to Part 5.
Gor. 21/9—8/11/41.**G.**
Gor. 30/4—27/5/44.**G.**
Gor. 26/8—12/10/46.**G.**
Gor. 16/6—22/9/47.**H.**
Gor. 24—27/2/48.**N/C.**
Gor. 20/2—2/4/49.**G.**
Gor. 27/9—24/11/51.**G.**
Gor. 27/11—12/12/51.**N/C.**
Gor. 9—18/4/53.**C/L.**
Gor. 22/3—8/5/54.**G.**
Gor. 3—7/1/56.**C/L.**
Gor. 31/1—16/3/57.**G.**
Rebuilt to Part 8.
Gor. 10/6—3/7/59.**H/I.**
Gor. 23/5—4/8/62.**G.**

BOILERS:
1210.
872 15/7/32.
1493 23/2/35.
3304 24/7/37.
3653 17/9/39.
3652 27/5/44.
3654 12/10/46.
3652 2/4/49.
3652 reno.22344 24/11/51.
28341 *(exO1 63630)* 16/3/57.
28806 *(ex63613)* 4/8/62.

SHEDS:
Immingham 30/9/27.
Doncaster 21/10/40.
Frodingham 25/7/43.
Doncaster 10/10/65.

RENUMBERED:
6592 1/10/27.
3788 12/10/46.

E**3788** 27/2/48.
63788 2/4/49.

CONDEMNED: 2/1/66.
Sold for scrap to T.W. Ward, Beighton, 2/66.

6593

N.B. Loco. 21864 7/1918.

M of M 1887.

To traffic 21/7/28.

REPAIRS:
Gor. 14/4—14/7/28.**G.**
Gor. 12/4—17/6/30.**G.**
Gor. 18/4/31.**L.**
Gor. 6—13/6/31.**L.**
Gor. 30/7—13/8/32.**G.**
Gor. 11—18/5/35.**G.**
Gor. 12/6—3/7/37.**G.**
Gor. 15/7—12/8/39.**G.**
Gor. 11—20/9/41.**G.**

BOILERS:
1282.
1968 13/8/32.
1205 18/5/35.
1962 3/7/37.
940 12/8/39.
3436 20/9/41.

SHEDS:
New England 21/7/28.
March 15/3/32.
Cambridge 9/6/32.
Doncaster 14/4/36.

RENUMBERED:
6593 14/7/28.

WITHDRAWN: 13/9/41.
Reno.745 and sent to Mid. East via Ellesmere Port, 17/10/41.

6594

N.B. Loco. 21869 2/1918.

M of M 1892.

To traffic 7/6/28.

REPAIRS:
Gor. 17/3—9/6/28.**G.**
Gor. 1/3—5/4/30.**G.**
Gor. 5—19/12/31.**G.**

Gor. 13—27/1/34.**G.**
Gor. 4—18/4/36.**G.**
Gor. 19—26/3/38.**G.**
Gor. 20—27/7/40.**G.**
Gor. 29/10—13/11/43.**G.**
Gor. 23/11—28/12/46.**G.**
Gor. 23/7—6/8/49.**G.**
Gor. 15/3—5/4/52.**G.**
Gor. 29/1—26/2/55.**G.**
Gor. 9/3/59. *Not repaired.*

BOILERS:
1887.
1066 19/12/31.
1358 27/1/34.
C1469 18/4/36.
3233 26/3/38.
867 27/7/40.
512 13/11/43.
3380 28/12/46.
1852 6/8/49.
22258 5/4/52.
22173 26/2/55.

SHEDS:
Doncaster 7/6/28.
GWR. 21/11/40.
Woodford 4/2/43.
Gorton 10/3/43.
West Hartlepool 20/3/43.
Colwick 20/1/44.
Doncaster 23/1/44.
Darnall 25/6/45.

RENUMBERED:
6594 9/6/28.
3790 26/5/46.
63790 6/8/49.

CONDEMNED: 12/3/59.
Cut up at Gorton.

6595

N.B. Loco. 21876 2/1918.

M of M 1899.

To traffic 20/9/27.

REPAIRS:
Gor. 11/6—17/9/27.**G.**
Gor. 18/1—22/2/30.**G.**
Gor. 14—28/11/31.**G.**
Gor. 8—22/7/33.**G.**
Gor. 23—30/11/35.**G.**
Gor. 26/2—12/3/38.**G.**
Gor. 20/7—3/8/40.**G.**
Gor. 19/4—10/5/41.**L.**
Gor. 28/10/43.

WORKS CODES:- Bpk - Beyer, Peacock. Crw - Crewe. Cw - Cowlairs. Dar- Darlington. Dby - Derby. Don - Doncaster. Ghd - Gateshead. Gor - Gorton. Inv - Inverurie. Str - Stratford.
REPAIR CODES:- **C/H** - Casual Heavy. **C/L** - Casual Light. **G** - General. **H** - Heavy. **H/I** - Heavy Intermediate. **L** - Light. **L/I** - Light Intermediate. **N/C** - Non-Classified.

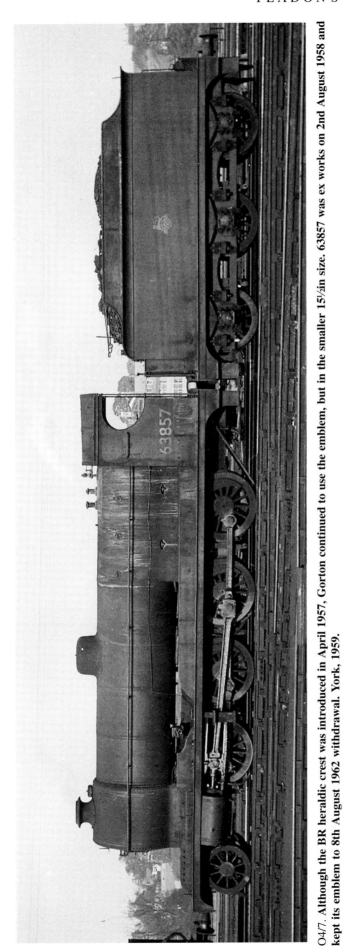

O4/7. Although the BR heraldic crest was introduced in April 1957, Gorton continued to use the emblem, but in the smaller 15½in size. 63857 was ex works on 2nd August 1958 and kept its emblem to 8th August 1962 withdrawal. York, 1959.

O4/7. The crest was applied to some Part 7, 63848 having it when ex works on 5th November 1959.

O4/7. Part 7 became extinct on 19th December 1965 when 63770 was withdrawn. It had a flat top dome, its boiler being the last 15D built - in October 1943.

6595 continued/.
Rebuilt to Class O1.

BOILERS:
1177.
1861 28/11/31.
1463 22/7/33.
1303 30/11/35.
1284 12/3/38.
3218 3/8/40.

SHEDS:
Langwith Jct. 20/9/27.
Doncaster 20/2/30.
GWR. 23/11/40.
Woodford 4/2/43.
Gorton 10/3/43.
West Hartlepool 20/3/43.

RENUMBERED:
6595 17/9/27.

_____

6596

N.B. Loco. 21879 3/1918.

M of M 1902.

To traffic 10/2/28.

REPAIRS:
Gor. 15/10/27—11/2/28.**G.**
Gor. 11/1—8/2/30.**G.**
Gor. 12—31/12/31.**G.**
Gor. 30/6—14/7/34.**G.**
Wakefield 2C mech. lub. fitted.
Gor. 11—25/7/36.**G.**
Gor. 13—20/8/38.**G.**
Gor. 11—25/1/41.**G.**
Gor. 4—19/12/42.**G.**
Gor. 2/2/46.
Rebuilt to Class O1.

BOILERS:
1265.
 486 31/12/31.
1015 14/7/34.
1325 25/7/36.
 856 20/8/38.
3430 25/1/41.
1271 19/12/42.

SHEDS:
Doncaster 10/2/28.
Tuxford 4/8/39.

RENUMBERED:
6596 11/2/28.

_____

6597

N.B. Loco. 21880 3/1918.

M of M 1903.

To traffic 23/7/27.

REPAIRS:
Gor. 16/4—23/7/27.**G.**
Gor. 17/8—28/9/29.**G.**
Gor. 19/3—2/4/32.**G.**
Gor. ?/?—22/9/34.**G.**
'Empire' twin plunger lub. to axles.
Gor. 5—19/12/36.**G.**
Gor. 11—18/2/39.**G.**
Gor. 4—23/8/41.**G.**

BOILERS:
1113.
1448 2/4/32.
 945 22/9/34.
3269 19/12/36.
 931 18/2/39.
3367 23/8/41.

SHED:
Langwith Jct. 23/7/27.

RENUMBERED:
6597 23/7/27.

WITHDRAWN: 13/9/41.
Reno.707 and sent to Middle East via Glasgow, 16/9/41.

_____

6598

N.B. Loco. 21885 3/1918.

M of M 1908.

To traffic 30/9/27.

REPAIRS:
Gor. 13/8—30/9/27.**G.**
Gor. 10/2—4/4/30.**G.**
Gor. 27/5—15/7/32.**G.**
Gor. 11/7—4/8/34.**G.**
Gor. 29/12/34—16/2/35.**L.**
Gor. 1/9—3/10/36.**G.**
Fountain lub. to axles.
Gor. 24/7—24/9/38.**G.**
Gor. 24/10—23/11/40.**G.**
Gor. 29/7—5/9/42.**G.**
Gor. 19/10—18/11/44.**G.**
Gor. 6/10/46—8/1/47.**G.**
Gor. 30/8—9/10/48.**G.**
Gor. 22/2—7/4/51.**G.**
Gor. 10—13/4/51.**N/C.**
Gor. 30/1—8/3/52.**C/H.**
Gor. 26/9—17/10/53.**G.**
Gor. 20—28/10/53.**N/C.**

Gor. 11—25/3/54.**N/C.**
Gor. 10/5—18/8/56.**G.**
Rebuilt to Part 8.
Gor. 24/2—25/3/60.**H/I.**
Gor. 30/3—5/4/60.**N/C.**

BOILERS:
1208.
1247 15/7/32.
1231 4/8/34.
1270 3/10/36.
1350 24/9/38.
3344 23/11/40.
3266 5/9/42.
3251 18/11/44.
3352 9/10/48.
22173 7/4/51.
22252 8/3/52.
22122 17/10/53.
28898 *(new)* 18/8/56.

SHEDS:
Colwick 30/9/27.
Langwith Jct. 31/10/27.
Colwick 27/10/46.
Annesley 12/10/47.
Colwick 8/2/48.
Annesley 14/11/48.
Colwick 11/9/49.
Annesley 2/9/51.
Colwick 4/11/51.
Staveley 20/7/52.
Colwick 22/9/52.
Staveley 5/10/52.
Langwith Jct. 29/11/59.

RENUMBERED:
  6598 30/9/27.
  3801 1/9/46.
  63801 9/10/48.

CONDEMNED: 16/7/63.
Into Don. for cut up 22/8/63.

_____

6599

N.B. Loco. 21888 4/1918.

M of M 1911.

To traffic 26/7/27.

REPAIRS:
Gor. 30/4—30/7/27.**G.**
Gor. 12/10—9/11/29.**G.**
Gor. 7—21/5/32.**G.**
Gor. 25/5—8/6/35.**G.**
Gor. 5—19/6/37.**G.**
Gor. 30/9—14/10/39.**G.**
Gor. 6—20/9/41.**G.**

BOILERS:
1125.
 809 21/5/32.

1937 8/6/35.
 853 19/6/37.
3299 14/10/39.
3372 20/9/41

SHEDS:
Sheffield 26/7/27.
Staveley 19/1/34.
Annesley 22/2/37.

RENUMBERED:
6599 30/7/27.

WITHDRAWN: 19/9/41.
Reno.734 and sent to Middle East via Greenock, 9/10/41.

_____

6600

N.B. Loco. 21891 5/1918.

M of M 1914.

To traffic 30/4/29.

REPAIRS:
Gor. 2/2—4/5/29.**G.**
Gor. 24/10—7/11/31.**G.**
Gor. 25/11—9/12/33.**G.**
Gor. 22/2—7/3/36.**G.**
Fountain lub. to axles.
Gor. 13—20/3/37.**H.**
Gor. 20/5—10/6/39.**G.**
Gor. 26/8—13/9/41.**G.**

BOILERS:
1219.
1489 7/11/31.
 825 9/12/33.
1126 7/3/36.
1228 20/3/37.
3372 10/6/39.
3434 13/9/41.

SHED:
Colwick 30/4/29.

RENUMBERED:
6600 4/5/29.

WITHDRAWN: 14/9/41.
Reno.718 and sent to Middle East via Birkenhead, 17/9/41.

_____

6601

N.B. Loco. 21892 5/1918.

M of M 1915.

To traffic 15/3/28.

6601 continued/.
REPAIRS:
Gor. 17/12/27—17/3/28.**G.**
Gor. 22/11—6/12/30.**G.**
Gor. 15—22/7/33.**G.**
Gor. 2—16/11/35.**G.**
Gor. 30/7—13/8/38.**G.**
Fountain lub. to axles.
Gor. 4—11/1/41.**G.**
Gor. 11—22/5/43.**G.**
Gor. 3/6/44.
Rebuilt to Class O1.

BOILERS:
  857.
1403 6/12/30.
1021 22/7/33.
  871 16/11/35.
3245 13/8/38.
3428 11/1/41.

SHEDS:
Colwick 15/3/28.
Doncaster 23/1/44.

RENUMBERED:
6601 17/2/28.

6602

N.B. Loco. 21897 5/1918.

M of M 1920.

To traffic 2/8/27.

REPAIRS:
Gor. 30/4—30/7/27.**G.**
Gor. 28/9—26/10/29.**G.**
Gor. 19/3—2/4/32.**G.**
Gor. 1—15/6/35.**G.**
Gor. 20/3—10/4/37.**G.**
Gor. 29/7—12/8/39.**G.**
Gor. 24/9—4/10/41.**G.**

BOILERS:
1141.
1858 2/4/32.
1285 15/6/35.
1456 10/4/37.
3303 12/8/39.
3215 4/10/41.

SHEDS:
Sheffield 2/8/27.
Staveley 31/1/34.

RENUMBERED:
6602 30/7/27.

WITHDRAWN: 4/10/41.
Reno.780 and sent to Mid. East.

6603

N.B. Loco. 21898 5/1918.

M of M 1921.

To traffic 21/1/28.

REPAIRS:
Gor. 8/10/27—28/1/28.**G.**
Gor. 15/2—15/3/30.**G.**
Gor. 18/6—2/7/32.**G.**
Gor. 17/11—1/12/34.**G.**
Gor. 26/1—2/2/35.**G.**
Gor. 27/2—6/3/37.**G.**
Gor. 15—29/7/39.**G.**
Gor. 2—18/10/41.**G.**

BOILERS:
1249.
1938 2/7/32.
1956 1/12/34.
1865 2/2/35.
3276 6/3/37.
1287 29/7/39.
3420 18/10/41.

SHEDS:
Sheffield 21/1/28.
Staveley 9/2/34.

RENUMBERED:
6603 28/1/28.

WITHDRAWN: 18/10/41.
Reno.789 and sent to Mid. East.

6604

N.B. Loco. 21902 6/1918.

M of M 1925.

To traffic 21/8/28.

REPAIRS:
Gor. 14/7—21/8/28.**G.**
Gor. 25/7—23/9/30.**G.**
Gor. 10/2—1/4/33.**G.**
Gor. 2/10—9/11/35.**G.**
Gor. 7/8—14/10/38.**G.**
Fountain lub. to axles.
Gor. 26/10—1/11/38.**N/C.**
Gor. 25/4—25/5/40.**G.**
Gor. 5—22/11/42.**G.**
Gor. 6—19/12/42.**N/C.**
Gor. 22/5—17/6/44.**L.**
Gor. 14/3—5/5/45.**G.**
Gor. 19/9—1/11/47.**G.**
Gor. 14/8—9/9/50.**G.**
Gor. 17—26/9/50.**N/C.**
Gor. 17/4—9/5/53.**G.**
Gor. 28/12/56—2/2/57.**G.**
Gor. 26/10—3/12/60.**H/I.**

Gor. 10—17/12/60.**N/C.**

BOILERS:
1275.
1162 1/4/33.
  924 9/11/35.
1399 14/10/38.
3249 25/5/40.
  934 22/11/42.
3297 5/5/45.
3212 (ex3797) 1/11/47.
22101 9/9/50.
22166 9/5/53.
22209 2/2/57.

SHEDS:
New England 21/8/28.
Grantham 19/1/31.
Doncaster 21/11/42.
Colwick 6/9/43.
Doncaster 23/1/44.
Frodingham 2/12/45.
Doncaster 7/4/46.
Mexborough 25/8/46.
Retford 22/9/63.
Staveley 10/1/65.

RENUMBERED:
  6604 21/8/28.
  3813 24/11/46.
63813 9/9/50.

CONDEMNED: 7/3/65.
*Sold for scrap to Arnott Young,
Parkgate, 5/65.*

6605

N.B. Loco. 21904 6/1918.

M of M 1927.

To traffic 17/1/28.

REPAIRS:
Gor. 8/10/27—21/1/28.**G.**
Gor. 3/5—7/6/30.**G.**
Gor. 14—21/5/32.**G.**
Gor. 22/9—6/10/34.**G.**
Gor. 24—31/10/36.**G.**
Gor. 8—22/7/39.**G.**
Don. 29/8—13/9/41.**G.**

BOILERS:
1263.
1340 7/6/30.
1290 21/5/32.
1154 6/10/34.
1872 31/10/36.
3282 22/7/39.

SHED:
Langwith Jct. 17/1/28.

RENUMBERED:
6605 21/1/28.

WITHDRAWN: 19/9/41.
Reno.764 and sent to Mid. East.

6606

N.B. Loco. 21906 6/1918.

M of M 1929.

To traffic 25/8/27.

REPAIRS:
Gor. 16/7—25/8/27.**G.**
Gor. 5/7—3/9/30.**G.**
Gor. 27/1—11/3/33.**G.**
Gor. 30/1—2/3/35.**G.**
Gor. 12/4—8/5/37.**G.**
Gor. 25/7—30/9/39.**G.**
Rebuilt to Part 5.
Gor. 23/3—10/5/41.**G.**
Gor. 13/11—11/12/43.**G.**
Gor. 9/11—8/12/45.**H.**
Gor. 17/9—6/11/48.**G.**
Gor. 26/6—11/8/51.**G.**
Gor. 24/9—14/11/53.**G.**
Gor. 8/9—3/12/55.**G.**
Rebuilt to Part 8.
Gor. 7—29/6/56.**N/C.**
Gor. 30/6—23/8/58.**C/H.**
Gor. 9/8—9/9/60.**G.**
Gor. 20—26/9/60.**G.**
Gor. 21/1/61—26/1/61.**N/C.**
Tender weatherboard fitted.

BOILERS:
1150.
1945 3/9/30.
1939 11/3/33.
1255 2/3/35.
1068 8/5/37.
3654 30/9/39.
3651 11/12/43.
1084 (ex6207) 8/12/45.
22341 11/8/51.
28886 (new) 3/12/55.
28933 (ex63840) 9/9/60.

SHEDS:
New England 25/8/27.
Grantham 31/5/35.
Colwick 10/9/35.
West Hartlepool 20/1/44.
Newport 5/10/44.
West Hartlepool 18/10/44.
Hull Springhead 12/1/45.
Hull Dairycoates 29/4/46.
Western Region 2/9/51.
Colwick 23/9/51.

RENUMBERED:
6606 25/8/27.

O4/8. It was not well appreciated that on all eight Parts of O4 class that the width over the running plate was 6½in. more adjacent to the cylinders, where it was 8ft 9½in. against 8ft 3in. elsewhere. On this photograph the wider part can be seen.

O4/8. Ten Part 8 engines were rebuilt from Part 1: 5388, 6205, 6228 (later renumbered 3613, 3738 and 3575), 63573, 63805, 63604, 63606, 63612, 63624 and 63683. All had their vacuum train braking equipment taken off. Gorton, 12th October 1947.

O4/8. From Part 2, five were rebuilt: 63644, 63647, 63653, 63674 and 63704. They lost the cut-down cab with which they had been fitted for service in Scottish Area, and the high front plate put on the tender by Cowlairs, except on 63644 which still had one as late as 16th May 1965. York shed, 11th October 1964.

O4/8. Part 8's major contributor was seventy-one of the ninety-nine from Part 3 as they required the least amount of alteration.

O4/8. Only one, No.3882, from Part 4 became Part 8, the frame extension under the cab being removed, but it differed from all the other Part 8 engines in retaining a curved rear end to its splashers. Mexborough shed, 20th August 1963.

6606 continued/.
3816 27/11/46.
63816 6/11/48.

CONDEMNED: 15/1/66.
*Sold for scrap to Geo. Cohen,
Kettering, 3/66.*

6607

N.B. Loco. 21916 8/1918.

M of M 1939.

To traffic 11/10/27.

REPAIRS:
Gor. 9/7—15/10/27.**G.**
Dar. 28/4—12/8/30.**G.**
Gor. 27/5—10/6/33.**G.**
Gor. 8—22/6/35.**G.**
Gor. 12—26/6/37.**G.**
Gor. 7—21/10/39.**G.**
Dar. 9—21/2/40.**N/C.**
Gor. 1—13/9/41.**G.**

BOILERS:
1200.
1966 10/6/33.
1277 22/6/35.
1115 *(ex6608)* 26/6/37.
1174 *(ex6634)* 21/10/39.
1964 13/9/41.

SHEDS:
Hull Dairycoates 11/10/27.
Hull Springhead 2/1/30.
Darlington 6/1/40.
Heaton 20/2/40.

RENUMBERED:
6607 15/10/27.

WITHDRAWN: 20/9/41.
*Reno.722 and sent to Middle
East via Glasgow, 8/10/41.*

6608

N.B. Loco. 22007 10/1918.

M of M 1949.

To traffic 30/6/28.

REPAIRS:
Gor. 31/3—30/6/28.**G.**
Dar. 27/6—16/9/30.**G.**
Gor. 24/12/32—7/1/33.**G.**
Gor. 23/9—7/10/33.**L.**
Gor. 23/3—6/4/35.**G.**
Gor. 5—19/6/37.**G.**
Gor. 3—24/2/40.**G.**

Gor. 24/3—4/4/42.**G.**
Gor. 10—17/6/44.**G.**
Gor. 29/6—3/8/46.**G.**
Gor. 24/5—21/6/47.**L.**
Gor. 14/8—11/9/48.**G.**
Gor. 18/8—8/9/51.**G.**
Gor. 19/12/53—16/1/54.**G.**
Gor. 19—27/1/54.**N/C.**
Gor. 28/9—2/11/57.**G.**
Rebuilt to Part 8.
Gor. 22/4—27/5/61.**H/I.**
Water treatment fitted.

BOILERS:
1948.
1005 7/1/33.
1115 6/4/35.
1254 19/6/37.
1004 24/2/40.
1225 *(ex6630)* 4/4/42.
862 17/6/44.
3291 *(ex6616)* 3/8/46.
1231 11/9/48.
22213 8/9/51.
22197 16/1/54.
28937 *(new)* 2/11/57.

SHEDS:
Hull Dairycoates 30/6/28.
Hull Springhead 2/1/30.
West Hartlepool 17/5/40.
Hull Dairycoates 5/3/45.
Western Region 2/9/51.
Immingham 16/9/51.
Tuxford 9/11/52.
Ardsley 27/9/53.

RENUMBERED:
6608 30/6/28.
3823 22/12/46.
63823 9/9/48.

CONDEMNED: 8/8/62.
Into Gor. for cut up 18/8/62.

6609

N.B. Loco. 22015 12/1918.

M of M 1957.

To Traffic 22/9/28.

REPAIRS:
Gor. 23/6—22/9/28.**G.**
Dar. 30/8—18/10/30.**G.**
Gor. 11/1—4/2/33.**G.**
Gor. 8/12/34—18/1/35.**G.**
Gor. 23/1—6/2/37.**G.**
Gor. 17/6—15/7/39.**G.**
Gor. 24/8—28/9/40.**G.**
Gor. 19/9—17/10/42.**G.**
Gor. 18—25/3/44.**L.**
Gor. 4/8—30/9/44.**G.**

Rebuilt to Part 8.
Gor. 20/6—17/8/46.**G.**
Gor. 10/8—16/9/48.**G.**
Gor. 20/3—28/4/51.**G.**
Gor. 29/6—13/8/54.**G.**
Gor. 9/6—2/8/58.**G.**
Gor. 19/10—23/11/62.**G.**
Dar. 15/12/64—20/2/65.**C/H.**

BOILERS:
1037.
1228 4/2/33.
1286 18/1/35.
3274 6/2/37.
3298 15/7/39.
3227 28/9/40.
1280 *(ex6553)* 17/10/42.
5023 *(new)* 30/9/44.
5079 *(ex3890)* 16/9/48.
28313 28/4/51.
28377 *(exO1 63646)* 13/8/54.
28396 *(exO1 63901)* 2/8/58.
28511 *(ex63858)* 23/11/62.

SHEDS:
Hull Dairycoates 22/9/28.
Hull Springhead 18/11/29.
Darlington 6/1/40.
Heaton 24/2/40.
Tyne Dock 23/7/45.
Hull Dairycoates 6/2/49.
Doncaster 2/9/51.
Mexborough 28/10/51.
Immingham 22/9/52.
Mexborough 5/10/52.
Langwith Jct. 3/9/61.

RENUMBERED:
6609 22/9/28.
3828 24/11/46.
63828 16/9/48.

CONDEMNED: 29/8/65.
*Sold for scrap to Garnham,
Harris & Elton, Chesterfield,
10/65.*

6610

N.B. Loco. 22020 1/1919.

M of M 1962.

To traffic 30/11/27.

REPAIRS:
Gor. 27/8—3/12/27.**G.**
Dar. 18/8—17/10/30.**G.**
Gor. 31/12/32—14/1/33.**G.**
Gor. 1—15/12/34.**G.**
Gor. 12—31/12/36.**G.**
Gor. 18/3—1/4/39.**G.**
Gor. 1—13/9/41.**G.**

BOILERS:
1852.
1142 14/1/33.
1107 15/12/34.
3271 31/12/36.
3267 1/4/39.
3234 13/9/41.

SHEDS:
Hull Dairycoates 30/11/27.
York 15/6/28.
Hull Springhead 4/11/29.
Heaton 24/2/40.

RENUMBERED:
6610 3/12/27.

WITHDRAWN: 20/9/41.
*Reno.729 and sent to Middle
East via Greenock, 8/10/41.*

6611

N.B. Loco. 22034 10/1918.

M of M 1976.

To traffic 27/10/27.

REPAIRS:
Gor. 30/7—29/10/27.**G.**
Dar. 16/12/29—29/3/30.**G.**
Gor. 26/11—10/12/32.**G.**
Gor. 1—8/12/34.**G.**
Gor. 3—17/10/36.**G.**
Gor. 10—17/6/39.**G.**
Gor. 22/2—8/3/41.**G.**
Gor. 14/11—5/12/42.**G.**
Gor. 4—18/11/44.**G.**
Gor. 8—29/12/45.**L.**
Gor. 15/3—19/4/47.**G.**
Gor. 21/8—4/9/48.**H.**
Gor. 26/11—17/12/49.**G.**
Gor. 27/10—24/11/51.**C/L.**
Gor. 9—23/8/52.**G.**
Gor. 26/8—9/9/52.**N/C.**
Gor. 1—8/8/53.**C/L.**
Gor. 11—12/8/53.**N/C.**
Gor. 12—26/6/54.**C/H.**
Gor. 29/6—2/7/54.**N/C.**
Gor. 21/5—2/7/55.**H/I.**
Gor. 14/2/59. *Not repaired.*

BOILERS:
1228.
1355 10/12/32.
1144 8/12/34.
1190 17/10/36.
1013 17/6/39.
1041 *(ex6625)* 8/3/41.
3252 *(ex6280)* 5/12/42.
3319 *(ex6578)* 18/11/44.
3380 *(ex3790)* 17/12/49.
3380 reno.22226 24/11/51.

6611 continued/.
22288 23/8/52.
22250 26/6/54.

SHEDS:
Hull Dairycoates 27/10/27.
York 15/6/28.
Bullcroft Jct. 29/10/29.
Hull Springhead 5/12/31.
Cudworth 12/1/34.
Heaton 12/6/40.
Tyne Dock 23/7/45.
Hull Dairycoates 6/2/49.
WR (Oxley) 2/9/51.
Colwick 23/9/51.
Gorton 21/3/54.
Colwick 4/7/54.
Mexborough 29/1/56.

RENUMBERED:
  6611 29/10/27.
  3835 12/10/46.
  63835 4/9/48.

CONDEMNED: 23/2/59.
Cut up at Gorton.

_____

6612

N.B. Loco. 22058 2/1919.

M of M 2000.

To traffic 11/8/28.

REPAIRS:
Gor. 12/5—11/8/28.**G.**
Dar. 30/8—25/10/30.**G.**
Gor. 10/12/32—24/1/33.**G.**
Gor. 13/10—3/11/34.**G.**
Gor. 6—27/2/37.**G.**
Gor. 13/12/39—3/2/40.**G.**
Rebuilt to Part 7.
Gor. 21/2—28/3/42.**G.**
Gor. 7—21/8/43.**H.**
Gor. 29/3—1/6/46.**G.**
Gor. 9/12/47—21/1/48.**H.**
Gor. 15/9—5/11/49.**G.**
Gor. 16/12/52—10/1/53.**G.**
Gor. 2/5—23/6/56.**G.**
Gor. 14/12/60—21/1/61.**H/I.**

BOILERS:
  1064.
  1188 24/1/33.
  1301 3/11/34.
  1286 27/2/37.
  3660 3/2/40.
  3663 *(ex6352)* 28/3/42.
  3696 *(new)* 21/8/43.
  3671 *(ex5350)* 1/6/46.
  3682 *(ex3748)* 24/1/48.
  3662 *(ex3857)* 5/11/49.
  22302 10/1/53.

22300 23/6/56.

SHEDS:
Hull Dairycoates 11/8/28.
Hull Springhead 23/10/29.
West Hartlepool 11/5/40.
Hull Dairycoates 5/3/45.
Cudworth 20/8/50.
Hull Dairycoates 1/1/51.
Doncaster 2/9/51.
Mexborough 28/10/51.
Langwith Jct. 1/3/64.

RENUMBERED:
  6612 11/8/28.
  3843 24/11/46.
  E3843 24/1/48.
  63843 5/11/49.

CONDEMNED: 7/11/65.
*Sold for scrap to Cox and
Danks, Wadsley Bridge, 12/65.*

_____

6613

N.B. Loco. 22059 2/1919.

M of M 2001.

To traffic 30/6/28.

REPAIRS:
Gor. 21/4—30/6/28.**G.**
Dar. 22/4—31/7/30.**G.**
Gor. 17—24/9/32.**G.**
Gor. 14/1—11/2/33.**L.**
Gor. 21/7—11/8/34.**G.**
Gor. 3—17/10/36.**G.**
Gor. 6—20/5/39.**G.**
Gor. 13—27/9/41.**G.**

BOILERS:
  1955.
  1158 24/9/32.
  1315 11/8/34.
  1206 17/10/36.
  3268 20/5/39.
  3267 27/9/41.

SHEDS:
Hull Dairycoates 30/6/28.
Hull Springhead 27/9/29.
Darlington 6/1/40.
Heaton 24/2/40.

RENUMBERED:
6613 30/6/28.

WITHDRAWN: 19/9/41.
*Reno.749 and sent to Middle
East via Glasgow, 18/10/41.*

_____

6614

N.B. Loco. 22137 5/1919.

M of M 2043.

To traffic 20/3/28.

REPAIRS:
Gor. 14/1—24/3/28.**G.**
Dar. 18/8—13/10/30.**G.**
Gor. 17/6—1/7/33.**G.**
Gor. 19/10—2/11/35.**G.**
Gor. 12—19/12/36.**L.**
Anti-vacuum valve leaking.
Gor. 21/5—4/6/38.**G.**
Gor. 9—16/11/40.**G.**
Gor. 24/7—1/8/42.**H.**
Gor. 21/12/43—8/1/44.**G.**
Gor. 21/12/46—11/1/47.**G.**
Gor. 23/7—6/8/49.**G.**
Gor. 15/3—5/4/52.**G.**
Gor. 21/8—2/10/54.**G.**
Gor. 5/10—13/11/54.**N/C.**
Gor. 12/4—10/5/58.**G.**
Gor. 13—18/5/58.**N/C.**
Gor. 29/5/61. *Not repaired.*

BOILERS:
  1304.
  1378 1/7/33.
  1864 2/11/35.
  3238 4/6/38.
  3312 16/11/40.
  1090 1/8/42.
  3217 8/1/44.
  807 11/1/47.
  3306 *(ex3862)* 6/8/49.
  22257 5/4/52.
  22263 2/10/54.
  22288 10/5/58.

SHEDS:
Hull Dairycoates 20/3/28.
Hull Springhead 23/10/29.
Hull Dairycoates 11/7/33.
Cudworth 4/12/35.
Heaton 28/3/43.
Tyne Dock 23/7/45.
Heaton 22/7/46.
Tyne Dock 8/9/46.
Hull Dairycoates 6/2/49.
Cudworth 12/11/50.
Royston 12/8/51.
Colwick 2/9/51.
Annesley 22/1/56.
Staveley 11/11/56.

RENUMBERED:
  6614 24/3/28.
  3845 17/11/46.
  63845 6/8/49.

CONDEMNED: 22/6/61.
Cut up at Gorton.

6615

N.B. Loco. 22141 6/1919.

M of M 2048.

To traffic 11/2/28.

REPAIRS:
Gor. 29/10/27—11/2/28.**G.**
Dar. 18/8—14/10/30.**G.**
Gor. 24/6—8/7/33.**G.**
Gor. 21/12/35—18/1/36.**G.**
Gor. 21/5—4/6/38.**G.**
Gor. 6—13/4/40.**G.**
Gor. 20/4—1/5/43.**G.**
Gor. 10—31/3/45.**G.**
Gor. 23/11—14/12/46.**G.**
Gor. 16/10—6/11/48.**G.**
Gor. 26/1—16/2/52.**G.**
Converted to oil fuel.

BOILERS:
  1268.
  1244 8/7/33.
  3227 18/1/36.
  3332 4/6/38.
  3235 13/4/40.
  3351 1/5/43.
  1280 *(ex6609)* 31/3/45.
  3271 *(ex6619)* 14/12/46.
  3251 *(ex3801)* 6/11/48.
  22242 16/2/52.

SHEDS:
Hull Dairycoates 11/2/28.
Hull Springhead 18/11/29.
Hull Dairycoates 11/7/33.
Cudworth 2/8/37.
Hull Springhead 29/4/38.
West Hartlepool 8/5/40.
Hull Springhead 5/1/45.
Hull Dairycoates 11/9/49.
Cudworth 16/10/49.
Royston 12/8/51.
Colwick 2/9/51.

RENUMBERED:
  6615 11/2/28.
  3849 14/12/46.
  63849 6/11/48.

SOLD TO W.D.: 22/2/52.
Reno.041 and sent to Egypt.

_____

6616

N.B. Loco. 22150 6/1919.

M of M 2059.

To traffic 29/10/27.

6616 continued/.
REPAIRS:
Gor. 30/7—29/10/27.**G.**
Dar. 12/6—15/9/30.**G.**
Gor. 22—29/4/33.**G.**
Gor. 8—22/6/35.**G.**
Gor. 12/6—3/7/37.**G.**
Gor. 13—20/4/40.**G.**
Gor. 9—28/2/42.**G.**
Gor. 28/2—18/3/44.**G.**
Gor. 1—22/6/46.**G.**
Gor. 14/8—4/9/48.**G.**
Gor. 12/5—2/6/51.**G.**
Gor. 14—21/3/53.**C/L.**
Tender changed.
Gor. 24—26/3/53.**N/C.**
Gor. 17—31/10/53.**H/I.**
Gor. 3—10/11/53.**N/C.**
Gor. 27/10—10/11/56.**C/L.**
Gor. 13—14/11/56.**N/C.**
Gor. 6—27/4/57.**C/H.**
Gor. 23/3/59. Not repaired.

BOILERS:
  1234.
  1027 29/4/33.
  1033 22/6/35.
  1106 3/7/37.
  1082 20/4/40.
  862 28/2/42.
  3291 (ex6344) 18/3/44.
  853 (ex6376) 22/6/46.
  3351 4/9/48.
  22190 2/6/51.
  22163 27/4/57.

SHEDS:
Hull Dairycoates 29/10/27.
Hull Springhead 24/3/30.
West Hartlepool 10/5/40.
Newport 5/10/44.
West Hartlepool 18/10/44.
Hull Springhead 10/1/45.
Hull Dairycoates 29/9/46.
Doncaster 2/9/51.

RENUMBERED:
  6616 29/10/27.
  3855 30/12/46.
  63855 4/9/48.

CONDEMNED: 31/3/59.
Cut up at Gorton.

———————————————

6617

N.B. Loco. 22153 6/1919.

M of M 2062.

To traffic 5/5/28.

REPAIRS:
Gor. 3/3—5/5/28.**G.**

Dar. 27/10—5/12/30.**G.**
Gor. 30/7—6/8/32.**G.**
Gor. 15—22/9/34.**G.**
Gor. 3—17/10/36.**G.**
Gor. 5—19/3/38.**G.**
Gor. 18/5—1/6/40.**G.**
Gor. 6—24/10/42.**G.**
Gor. 25/9—9/10/43.**G.**
Gor. 2—23/3/46.**G.**
Gor. 7—14/2/48.**H.**
Gor. 25/6/49.
Rebuilt to Class O1.

BOILERS:
  868.
  1016 6/8/32.
  1207 22/9/34.
  1231 17/10/36.
  3223 19/3/38.
  3216 1/6/40.
  3226 (ex6220) 24/10/42.
  1206 (ex6342) 9/10/43.
  3241 (ex6342) 23/3/46.

SHEDS:
York 5/5/28.
Hull Springhead 6/2/30.
York 2/10/40.
Heaton 28/3/43.
Tyne Dock 23/7/45.
Heaton 22/7/46.
Tyne Dock 8/9/46.

RENUMBERED:
  6617 5/5/28.
  3856 1/12/46.
  E**3856** 14/2/48.

———————————————

6618

N.B. Loco. 22154 7/1919.

M of M 2063.

To traffic 10/3/28.

REPAIRS:
Gor. 26/11/27—10/3/28.**G.**
Dar. 20/10—5/12/30.**G.**
Dar. 24/5/32. Not repaired.
Sent to Gorton.
Gor. 18/6—23/7/32.**G.**
Gor. 20/10—3/11/34.**G.**
Gor. 13—27/6/36.**G.**
Gor. 8—29/10/38.**G.**
Gor. 31/5—14/6/41.**G.**
Gor. 22/4—15/5/43.**G.**
Rebuilt to Part 7.
Gor. 22/12/45—12/1/46.**G.**
Gor. 26/4—17/5/47.**L.**
Gor. 21/5—18/6/49.**G.**
After collision.
Gor. 23/2—15/3/52.**G.**
Gor. 2/10—6/11/54.**G.**

Gor. 31/5—2/8/58.**G.**
Gor. 1/10—19/11/60.**C/L.**

BOILERS:
  858.
  1016 5/12/30.
  1286 23/7/32.
  1176 3/11/34.
  548 27/6/36.
  1075 29/10/38.
  929 14/6/41.
  3692 15/5/43.
  3662 (ex5405) 12/1/46.
  3670 18/6/49.
  22329 15/3/52.
  22332 6/11/54.
  22310 2/8/58.

SHEDS:
Hull Dairycoates 10/3/28.
Hull Springhead 18/11/29.
Darlington 6/1/40.
Heaton 24/2/40.
Tyne Dock 23/7/45.
Heaton 22/7/46.
Tyne Dock 8/9/46.
Hull Dairycoates 6/2/49.
Cudworth 12/11/50.
Royston 12/8/51.
Colwick 2/9/51.
Ardsley 22/9/52.
Wakefield 22/2/59.
Ardsley 11/6/61.

RENUMBERED:
  6618 10/3/28.
  3857 4/8/46.
  63857 18/6/49.

CONDEMNED: 8/8/62.
Into Gor. for cut up 10/62.

———————————————

6619

N.B. Loco. 22155 7/1919.

M of M 2064.

To traffic 30/6/27.

REPAIRS:
Gor. 4—30/6/27.**G.**
Gor. 25/9—25/11/29.**G.**
Gor. 11/7—20/8/32.**G.**
Gor. 13/1—1/2/36.**G.**
Intensifore removed.
Fountain lub. to axles.
Gor. 5—21/8/37.**G.**
Gor. 21/1—24/2/40.**G.**
Str. 5/8—28/9/42.**G.**
Gor. 23/8—16/9/44.**G.**
Gor. 21/7—7/9/46.**G.**
Gor. 18/12/47—5/2/48.**G.**
Gor. 18/10—27/11/48.**G.**

Gor. 26/10—25/11/50.**G.**
Gor. 10/3—9/5/53.**G.**
Rebuilt to Part 8.
Gor. 25/11—18/12/54.**C/L.**
Gor. 17/12/56—19/1/57.**G.**
Gor. 2—19/6/59.**C/L.**
Gor. 31/7—7/9/62.**G.**
In store 30/9/32—11/11/33.

BOILERS:
  1107.
  1189 20/8/32.
  1169 1/2/36.
  1058 21/8/37.
  1254 24/2/40.
  1235 28/9/42.
  3271 16/9/44.
  1005 7/9/46.
  3271 27/11/48.
  22134 25/11/50.
  28842 (new) 9/5/53.
  28511 (exB1 61137) 19/1/57.
  28341 (ex63788) 7/9/62.

SHEDS:
New England 30/6/27.
Colwick 14/11/33.
Langwith Jct. 1/12/40.
Colwick 27/10/46.
Annesley 6/2/49.
Gorton 26/11/50.
Doncaster 14/10/51.
Colwick 29/8/65.
Doncaster 26/12/65.

RENUMBERED:
  6619 30/6/27.
  3858 7/9/46.
  E**3858** 5/2/48.
  63858 27/11/48.

CONDEMNED: 17/4/66.
Sold for scrap to Station Steel,
Wath, 5/66.

———————————————

6620

N.B. Loco. 22156 7/1919.

M of M 2065.

To traffic 11/11/27.

REPAIRS:
Gor. 22/10—11/11/27.**G.**
Gor. 12/5—8/7/30.**G.**
Gor. 19/2—13/4/33.**G.**
Gor. 14/6—27/7/35.**G.**
Gor. 19/4—5/6/37.**G.**
Gor. 21/4—27/5/39.**G.**
Gor. 31/3—10/5/41.**G.**
Gor. 10/4—22/5/43.**G.**
Gor. 7/12/44—11/1/45.**G.**
Gor. 9/9—9/11/46.**G.**

O4/8. **From February 1955, as the Diagram 15A boilers wore out, four Part 5, 63628, 63726, 63788 and 63816 were changed to Part 8. The boiler and cab were their main changes but 63628 needed its rear sandboxes moving to outside the cab. Doncaster shed.**

O4/8. **Two from Part 6, which had originally been Class O5, Nos.63914 and 63915, also became Part 8, and changed to side window cab which they had not had previously. Retford, July 1962.**

6620 continued/.
Gor. 5/4—7/5/49.**G.**
Gor. 8/1—3/2/51.**C/H.**
Gor. 3/4—5/5/51.**C/H.**
Gor. 5—8/5/52.**C/L.**
Gor. 13/9—4/10/52.**G.**
Gor. 22/9—31/10/53.**C/L.**
Gor. 3—6/11/53.**N/C.**
Gor. 9/8—24/9/55.**G.**
Gor. 19/1—23/3/56.**C/L.**
Gor. 19/4—21/6/58.**C/H.**
Gor. 15/9—17/10/60.**G.**

BOILERS:
1214.
1325 8/7/30.
1057 13/4/33.
1959 27/7/35.
1013 5/6/37.
1377 *(ex Cow)* 27/5/39.
3355 10/5/41.
1940 22/5/43.
933 11/1/45.
3321 9/11/46.
1136 7/5/49.
1136 reno.22159 3/2/51.
22185 5/5/51.
22104 4/10/52.
22115 24/9/55.
22142 17/10/60.

SHEDS:
Doncaster 11/11/27.
Mexborough 25/11/27.
Annesley 23/2/29.
Staveley 16/6/49.
Annesley 17/9/50.
Gorton 26/11/50.
Colwick 13/6/54.

RENUMBERED:
6620 11/11/27.
3859 1/9/46.
63859 7/5/49.

CONDEMNED: 18/10/63.
*Sold for scrap to Round Oak
Steel, Brierly Hill, 1/64.*

6621

N.B. Loco. 22157 7/1919.

M of M 2066.

To traffic 29/9/27.

REPAIRS:
Gor. 25/6—24/9/27.**G.**
Gor. 12/10—16/11/29.**G.**

Gor. 14—21/5/32.**G.**
Gor. 25/5—1/6/35.**G.**
Gor. 18/9—2/10/37.**G.**
Gor. 10/2—9/3/40.**G.**
Rebuilt to Part 7.
Gor. 12—15/8/42.**L.**
Gor. 8—31/7/43.**G.**
Gor. 30/6—28/7/45.**G.**
Gor. 1—22/11/47.**G.**
Gor. 1—22/4/50.**G.**
Gor. 1—8/11/52.**G.**
Gor. 25/6—6/8/55.**G.**
Gor. 5/4—10/5/58.**G.**
Gor. 30/5—8/6/58.**N/C.**
Gor. 11—26/6/59.**N/C.**
Water treatment fitted.
Gor. 30/9/61. *Not repaired.*

BOILERS:
1207.
1866 21/5/32.
1417 1/6/35.
1852 2/10/37.
3662 9/3/40.
3676 31/7/43.
3668 28/7/45.
3669 22/11/47.
3679 22/4/50.
22304 8/11/52.
22871 6/8/55.
22317 10/5/58.

SHEDS:
Immingham 29/9/27.
GWR. 25/11/40.
Woodford 20/7/42.
Darnall 3/2/46.
Immingham 16/9/56.
Colwick 10/4/60.

RENUMBERED:
6621 24/9/27.
3860 26/5/46.
63860 22/4/50.

CONDEMNED: 5/10/61.
Cut up at Gorton.

6622

N.B. Loco. 22159 7/1919.

M of M 2068.

To traffic 19/10/27.

REPAIRS:
Gor. 27/8—19/10/27.**G.**
Gor. 7/6—18/7/29.**G.**
Gor. 4/4—4/6/31.**G.**

Gor. 17/7—2/9/33.**G.**
Gor. 8—21/3/36.**G.**
Intensifore removed.
Fountain lub. to axles.
Gor. 13/3—14/4/38.**G.**
Gor. 29/9—26/10/40.**G.**
Gor. 30/10/42—2/1/43.**G.**
Gor. 30/11/45—26/1/46.**G.**
Gor. 31/3—4/5/48.**G.**
Gor. 1—26/8/50.**G.**
Gor. 9—13/9/50.**N/C.**
Gor. 3—29/11/52.**G.**
Gor. 8/11—18/12/54.**G.**
Gor. 28/9—9/11/57.**G.**
Rebuilt to Part 8.
Gor. 2—16/8/58.**N/C.**
Gor. 20/9—26/10/60.**H/I.**

BOILERS:
1242.
1943 4/6/31.
515 2/9/33.
3235 21/3/36.
3326 14/4/38.
1858 26/10/40.
3338 2/1/43.
3429 26/1/46.
3330 4/5/48.
1070 26/8/50.
22133 29/11/52.
22281 18/12/54.
28938 *(new)* 9/11/57.

SHEDS:
Immingham 19/10/27.
Tuxford 21/1/30.
Langwith Jct. 27/9/53.

RENUMBERED:
6622 19/10/27.
3861 7/9/46.
63861 1/5/48.

CONDEMNED: 21/2/65.
*Sold for scrap to Arnott Young,
Parkgate, 4/65.*

6623

N.B. Loco. 22169 8/1919.

M of M 2078.

To traffic 6/4/27.

REPAIRS:
Gor. 12/2—2/4/27.**G.**
Gor. 26/10—30/11/29.**G.**
Gor. 9—23/7/32.**G.**
Gor. 22/12/34—12/1/35.**G.**

Intensifore removed.
Gor. 16—23/1/37.**G.**
Gor. 15—29/4/39.**G.**
Gor. 11—23/8/41.**G.**

BOILERS:
1002.
1106 23/7/32.
1319 12/1/35.
1259 23/1/37.
1964 29/4/39.
3378 23/8/41.

SHED:
Woodford 6/4/27.

RENUMBERED:
6623 2/4/27.

WITHDRAWN: 13/9/41.
*Reno.716 and sent to Middle
East via Glasgow, 15/9/41.*

6624

N.B. Loco. 22170 8/1919.

M of M 2079.

To traffic 16/8/28.

REPAIRS:
Gor. 26/5—18/8/28.**G.**
Gor. 2—23/5/31.**G.**
Gor. 26/8—2/9/33.**G.**
Gor. 8—22/2/36.**G.**
Intensifore removed.
Fountain lub. to axles.
Gor. 30/7—6/8/38.**G.**
Gor. 7—14/12/40.**G.**
Str. 8/9—28/11/42.**G.**
Gor. 27/7—14/8/43.**L.**
Gor. 13—15/4/44.**L.**
Tender repairs.
Gor. 1/7/44.
Rebuilt to Class O1.

BOILERS:
924.
154 23/5/31.
1069 2/9/33.
1198 22/2/36.
3225 6/8/38.
3339 14/12/40.
3405 28/11/42.

SHEDS:
Colwick 16/8/28.
Doncaster 23/1/44.

WORKS CODES:- Bpk - Beyer, Peacock. Crw - Crewe. Cw - Cowlairs. Dar- Darlington. Dby - Derby. Don - Doncaster. Ghd - Gateshead. Gor - Gorton. Inv - Inverurie. Str - Stratford.
REPAIR CODES:- **C/H** - Casual Heavy. **C/L** - Casual Light. **G** - General. **H** - Heavy. **H/I** - Heavy Intermediate. **L** - Light. **L/I** - Light Intermediate. **N/C** - Non-Classified.

172

(above) O4/8. **Between August 1954 and March 1956 four Diagram 15D boilers on Part 7 engines were condemned and others were coming to the end of their economic life. Starting with 63706, ex works on 24th November 1956, justification was found for rebuilding six Part 7 to Part 8, Nos.63655, 63675, 63705, 63794 and 63884 being the others by August 1958. Staveley, April 1965.**

(right) O4/8. **Rebuilding to Part 8 involved fitting a Diagram 100A boiler, and a cab with two side windows. The former needed a saddle to carry the circular smokebox and as the new cab was 4in. wider there was no difficulty with the screw reverser. The eleven rebuilt in 1944 had their original numbers but just NE on the tender. Gorton shed.**

O4/8. **Between April 1946 and October 1947 the above eleven had LNER restored and by 1st January 1946 had acquired Thompson renumbering. No.6205 ran as No.3552 from 22nd November 1946 to 16th February 1947 when it became 63738. The five added in 1947, Nos.3633, 3651, 3653, 3818, 3882 all had LNER and number applied in shaded transfers.**

O4/8. From February 1948 BRITISH RAILWAYS in Gill sans painted and unshaded was put on the tender and 63818, ex works on 17th September 1949, was probably the last O4/8 to get lettering. The E prefix was carried by E3575 (14th) and E3893 (17th), both in February 1948, and from 19th May 1948 on 63738 the full BR number was applied. Gorton works, 25th September 1949.

O4/8. From late 1949 to 1957, the large (28in.) size emblem was put on , 63877 getting it when it became Part 8, ex works on 27th April 1957. Staveley, 17th August 1957.

6624 continued/.
RENUMBERED:
6624 18/8/28.

6625

N.B. Loco. 22172 8/1919.

M of M 2081.

To traffic 19/4/27.

REPAIRS:
Gor. 12/2—16/4/27.**G.**
Gor. 10/8—14/9/29.**G.**
Gor. 28/11—19/12/31.**G.**
Gor. 3—17/3/34.**G.**
*Spring gear altered for working
to Whitemoor.*
Gor. 30/11—14/12/35.**G.**
Intensifore removed.
Gor. 21/5—4/6/38.**G.**
Gor. 8—29/7/39.**L.**
Gor. 1—8/2/41.**G.**
Gor. 27/12/41—17/1/42.**L.**
Gor. 17/2—6/3/43.**G.**
Gor. 22—29/7/44.**L.**
Gor. 9/12/44.
Rebuilt to Class O1.

BOILERS:
1004.
1758 19/12/31.
1458 17/3/34.
1967 14/12/35.
1041 4/6/38.
 815 8/2/41.
1041 6/3/43.

SHEDS:
Gorton 19/4/27.
Doncaster 13/11/31.
Gorton 4/12/31.

RENUMBERED:
6625 16/4/27.

6626

N.B. Loco. 22173 8/1919.

M of M 2082.

To traffic 16/6/27.

REPAIRS:
Gor. 26/3—18/6/27.**G.**
Gor. 16/11—14/12/29.**G.**
Gor. 11—25/6/32.**G.**
Gor. 16—30/6/34.**G.**
Gor. 17—31/10/36.**G.**
Intensifore removed.
Fountain lub. to axles.

Gor. 14—28/1/39.**G.**
Gor. 27/4—11/5/40.**G.**
Gor. 30/7—8/8/42.**G.**
Gor. 27/9/44.
Rebuilt to Class O1.

BOILERS:
1078.
1365 25/6/32.
1136 30/6/34.
 931 31/10/36.
1464 28/1/39.
 865 11/5/40.
3401 8/8/42.

SHEDS:
Woodford 16/6/27.
Doncaster 24/9/28.
Mexborough 1/10/28.
Woodford 19/11/28.
Colwick 13/10/40.
Doncaster 23/1/44.

RENUMBERED:
6626 18/6/27.

6627

N.B. Loco. 22175 9/1919.

M of M 2084.

To traffic 17/5/27.

REPAIRS:
Gor. 26/2—21/5/27.**G.**
Gor. 10/8—14/9/29.**G.**
Gor. 15—29/8/31.**G.**
Gor. 23/9—7/10/33.**G.**
Gor. 9—16/11/35.**G.**
Intensifore removed.
Gor. 7—14/11/36.**G.**
Gor. 30/9—14/10/39.**G.**
Str. 1/9—17/10/42.**G.**
Gor. 19—22/7/44.**L.**
Tender only.
Gor. 9—30/6/45.**G.**
Gor. 10—31/1/48.**G.**
Gor. 10—31/3/51.**G.**
Gor. 4—15/9/51.**C/L.**
Gor. 9—30/5/53.**G.**
Gor. 3—13/6/53.**N/C.**
Gor. 22/5—12/6/54.**C/L.**
Gor. 10—16/6/54.**N/C.**
Gor. 17/3—21/4/56.**G.**
Gor. 28—30/4/56.**N/C.**
Gor. 22—29/3/58.**C/L.**
After collision.
Gor. 4/10—1/11/58.**G.**
Water treatment fitted.
Gor. 23/1/62. *Not repaired.*

BOILERS:
1018.

1243 29/8/31.
1011 7/10/33.
1221 16/11/35.
1340 14/11/36.
1019 14/10/39.
1254 17/10/42.
3405 30/6/45.
3415 31/1/48.
22172 31/3/51.
22136 30/5/53.
22151 21/4/56.
22874 1/11/58.

SHEDS:
Gorton 17/5/27.
Brunswick 29/11/35.
Gorton 14/11/36.
Grantham 2/5/37.
Mexborough 21/11/42.
Doncaster 27/8/44.
Mexborough 25/8/46.
Langwith Jct. 2/7/50.

RENUMBERED:
6627 21/5/27.
3870 28/7/46.
ᴇ**3870** 31/1/48.
63870 31/3/51.

CONDEMNED: 26/1/62.
Cut up at Gorton.

6628

N.B. Loco. 22177 10/1919.

M of M 2087.

To traffic 29/4/27.

REPAIRS:
Gor. 12/2—30/4/27.**G.**
Gor. 24/8—28/9/29.**G.**
Gor. 21/11—5/12/31.**G.**
Gor. 21/4—5/5/34.**G.**
Gor. 6—20/6/36.**G.**
Intensifore removed.
Fountain lub. to axles.
Gor. 25/2—11/3/39.**G.**
Gor. 30/9—18/10/41.**G.**

BOILERS:
1001.
1367 5/12/31.
 821 5/5/34.
3247 20/6/36.
3264 11/3/39.
3303 18/10/41.

SHEDS:
Gorton 29/4/27.
Grantham 4/5/37.

RENUMBERED:
6628 30/4/27.

WITHDRAWN: 18/10/41.
Reno.786 and sent to Mid. East.

6629

N.B. Loco. 22185 5/1919.

M of M 2095.

To traffic 24/11/27.

REPAIRS:
Gor. 22/10—24/11/27.**G.**
Gor. 21—28/12/29.**G.**
Gor. 16—?/7/32.**G.**
Gor. 4/4—?/4/35.**G.**
Gor. 30/7—14/8/37.**G.**
Don. 17—22/7/39.**L.**
Gor. 17—?/2/40.**G.**
Gor. 29/7—5/9/42.**G.**
Gor. 17/8—16/9/44.**G.**
Gor. 7/12/46—18/1/47.**G.**
Gor. 25/10—4/12/48.**G.**
Gor. 14/9—14/10/50.**G.**
Gor. 8/10—1/11/52.**G.**
Gor. 16/6—20/8/55.**G.**
Rebuilt to Part 8.
Gor. 2/9—5/10/57.**C/H.**
Gor. 1—16/11/57.**N/C.**
Gor. 22/4—19/5/59.**G.**
Gor. 25/1—27/2/62.**G.**

BOILERS:
1215.
 828 ?/7/32.
1481 ?/4/35.
1305 14/8/37.
3385 ?/2/40.
3312 5/9/42.
3214 16/9/44.
3217 18/1/47.
3299 4/12/48.
22118 14/10/50.
22875 1/11/52.
28882 *(new)* 20/8/55.
28338 *(ex63644)* 5/10/57.
28895 *(ex63785)* 19/5/59.
28303 *(exO1 63808)* 27/2/62.

SHEDS:
Immingham 24/11/27.
Tuxford 7/2/34.
Immingham 7/5/34.
GWR. 22/11/40.
Woodford 21/7/42.
Staveley 3/4/44.
Annesley 12/10/47.
Gorton 26/11/50.
Colwick 13/6/54.

6629 continued/.
RENUMBERED:
 6629 24/11/27.
 3873 30/6/46.
 63873 4/12/48.

CONDEMNED: 15/1/66.
*Sold for scrap to Geo. Cohen,
Kettering, 3/66.*

6630

N.B. Loco. 22186 6/1919.

M of M 2096.

To traffic 10/3/28.

REPAIRS:
Gor. 12/12/27—10/3/28.**G.**
Dar. 15/5—13/8/30.**G.**
Dar. 13/1—8/2/32.**G.**
Gor. 13—27/1/34.**G.**
Gor. 23/11—7/12/35.**G.**
Gor. 8—22/1/38.**G.**
Gor. 4—11/5/40.**G.**
Gor. 4—14/3/42.**G.**
Gor. 23/3/44.
Rebuilt to Class O1.

BOILERS:
1286.
1318 8/2/32.
1967 27/1/34.
 864 7/12/35.
1118 22/1/38.
1225 *(ex6633)* 11/5/40.
1082 *(ex6616)* 14/3/42.

SHEDS:
Hull Dairycoates 10/3/28.
Hull Springhead 7/4/30.
Heaton 6/7/40.

RENUMBERED:
 6630 10/3/28.

6631

N.B. Loco. 22194 6/1919.

M of M 2104.

To traffic 26/5/28.

REPAIRS:
Gor. 5—26/5/28.**G.**
Dar. 8/12/30—28/1/31.**G.**
Gor. 18—25/3/33.**G.**
Gor. 31/1—9/2/35.**G.**
Gor. 9—19/12/36.**G.**
Gor. 5/7—3/8/38.**G.**
Gor. 20/2—11/3/40.**G.**

Gor. 20/2—22/3/41.**L.**
Gor. 22—25/7/34.**L.**
Gor. 13/4—9/5/42.**G.**
Gor. 7—27/5/44.**G.**
Gor. 27/8—9/10/47.**G.**
Gor. 18/4—13/5/50.**G.**
Gor. 17—22/5/50.**N/C.**
Gor. 22/8—8/9/51.**C/L.**
Gor. 11—12/9/51.**N/C.**
Gor. 13/8—6/9/52.**G.**
Gor. 10/1—26/2/55.**G.**
Gor. 8/7—7/9/57.**G.**
Rebuilt to Part 8.
Gor. 11—20/12/58.**N/C.**
Gor. 19/6—10/7/59.**C/L.**
Gor. 30/9—4/11/61.**L/I.**

BOILERS:
1876.
 861 28/1/31.
 822 25/3/33.
1680 9/2/35.
 863 19/12/36.
1314 3/8/38.
1365 11/3/40.
 949 9/5/42.
1259 27/5/44.
3383 9/10/47.
3339 13/5/50.
22292 6/9/52.
22128 26/2/55.
28935 *(new)* 7/9/57.

SHEDS:
York 26/5/28.
Hull Springhead 21/8/30.
West Hartlepool 7/5/40.
Immingham 11/6/44.
Colwick 23/9/62.
Retford 30/12/62.
Staveley 10/1/65.

RENUMBERED:
 6631 26/5/28.
 3878 22/6/46.
 63878 13/5/50.

CONDEMNED: 14/3/65.
*Sold for scrap to Steel
Breaking & Dismantling,
Chesterfield, 5/65.*

6632

N.B. Loco. 22206 7/1919.

M of M 2116.

To traffic 17/3/28.

REPAIRS:
Gor. 14/1—17/3/28.**G.**
Dar. 26/9—12/11/30.**G.**
Gor. 26/11—3/12/32.**G.**

Gor. 22/12/34—5/1/35.**G.**
Gor. 20/6—4/7/36.**G.**
Gor. 11—25/2/39.**G.**
Gor. 26/4—17/5/41.**G.**
Gor. 22/7—7/8/43.**G.**
Gor. 3—17/11/45.**G.**
Gor. 15—30/8/47.**L.**
Tender only.
Gor. 10—24/4/48.**G.**
Gor. 11—25/11/50.**G.**
Gor. 20/12/52—10/1/53.**G.**
Gor. 22/1—19/2/55.**G.**
Gor. 5/7—30/8/58.**G.**
Rebuilt to Part 8.
Gor. 27/9—3/10/58.**N/C.**
Gor. 1—15/8/59.**C/L.**

BOILERS:
 859.
1680 3/12/32.
1856 5/1/35.
 821 4/7/36.
1869 17/5/41.
3413 *(ex6328)* 7/8/43.
3252 17/11/45.
3361 *(exC4 2924)* 24/4/48.
22132 25/11/50.
22891 10/1/53.
22271 19/2/55.
28972 *(new)* 30/8/58.

SHEDS:
Hull Dairycoates 17/3/28.
Hull Springhead 7/4/30.
Cudworth 15/7/35.
York 2/10/40.
Heaton 28/3/43.
Tyne Dock 23/7/45.
Heaton 22/7/46.
Tyne Dock 8/9/46.
Hull Dairycoates 6/2/49.
Western Region 2/9/51.
Immingham 16/9/51.
Colwick 20/9/53.
Darnall 21/3/54.
Langwith Jct. 16/9/62.
Darnall 23/9/62.

RENUMBERED:
 6632 17/3/28.
 3881 8/9/46.
 63881 24/4/48.

CONDEMNED: 9/12/62.
Into Dby. for cut up 8/63.

6633

N.B. Loco. 22216 8/1919.

M of M 2126.

To traffic 24/5/27.

REPAIRS:
Gor. 30/4—24/5/27.**G.**
Gor. 13—20/7/29.**G.**
Gor. 11—?/7/31.**G.**
Gor. 25/11—?/12/33.**G.**
Gor. 18/11—5/12/35.**G.**
Gor. 27/10—?/11/37.**G.**
Gor. 12—20/4/40.**G.**
Rebuilt to Part 7.
Gor. 26/1—26/2/43.**G.**
Gor. 19/1—10/3/45.**G.**
Gor. 25/10—2/12/47.**G.**
Gor. 16/12/49—2/2/50.**C/L.**
Gor. 5/11—2/12/50.**G.**
Gor. 6—7/12/50.**N/C.**
Gor. 28/6—9/8/52.**G.**
Gor. 4/10—6/11/54.**G.**
Gor. 13/12/56—9/2/57.**G.**
Rebuilt to Part 8.
Gor. 7/3—9/4/60.**H/I.**
Gor. 12—27/4/60.**N/C.**
Gor. 22/3—19/4/62.**C/L.**

BOILERS:
1035.
1168 ?/7/31.
1960 ?/12/33.
1859 5/12/35.
1225 ?/11/37.
3665 20/4/40.
3687 26/2/43.
3666 10/3/45.
3684 2/12/47.
22310 2/12/50.
22305 9/8/52.
22331 6/11/54.
28832 *(exO1 63712)* 9/2/57.

SHEDS:
Gorton 24/5/27.
Doncaster 8/1/38.
Immingham 17/1/38.
GWR. 23/11/40.
Woodford 12/1/43.
Thornton Jct. 25/1/43.
Doncaster 2/10/43.
Ardsley 11/6/44.
Mexborough 18/8/46.
Doncaster 20/10/47.
Langwith Jct. 25/6/50.
Staveley 2/12/51.
Mexborough 31/1/60.
Frodingham 3/12/61.

RENUMBERED:
 6633 24/5/27.
 3884 10/11/46.
 63884 2/2/50.

CONDEMNED: 9/6/64.
*Sold for scrap to T.W. Ward,
Beighton, 8/64.*

O4/8. **Instead of changing to the BR crest, available from May 1957, Gorton first switched to using up the smaller emblem. This was put on 63861 when rebuilt to Part 8, ex works on 9th November 1957, and 63781 to Part 8 on 19th April 1958, also had the small emblem.**

O4/8. **By April 1959 Gorton had begun to use the 1957 BR crest and 63631, ex works on 12th December 1959, had it. Northwich shed, 3rd April 1961.**

177

O4/8. Gorton continued to give general repairs to Part 8 engines until 63819 was ex works on 3rd January 1963. Curiously 63828 was given a casual/heavy repair at Darlington, as late as 15th December 1964 to 20th February 1965 and it was then withdrawn on 29th August 1965. 63877 was ex Gorton on 12th August 1961 as shown - note that it had electrification-warning flashes put on.

O4/8. The last four of Part 8 Nos.63653, 63781, 63818, 63858 were all withdrawn on 17th April 1966 from Doncaster shed, making the whole of Class O4 extinct. Gorton, April 1959.

6634

N.B. Loco. 22222 9/1919.

M of M 2132.

To traffic 24/7/28.

REPAIRS:
Gor. 5/5—21/7/28.**G.**
Gor. 21/2—7/3/31.**G.**
Gor. 11—18/11/33.**G.**
Gor. 21/9—12/10/35.**G.**
Gor. 14—21/8/37.**G.**
Gor. 7—14/10/39.**G.**
Gor. 9—31/1/42.**G.**
Str. 13/7—13/8/42.**L.**
Gor. 9—20/11/43.**G.**
Gor. 20/4—11/5/46.**G.**
Gor. 5—19/6/48.**G.**
Gor. 21/10—4/11/50.**G.**
Gor. 4—25/4/53.**G.**
Gor. 28—30/4/53.**N/C.**
Gor. 8—13/5/53.**N/C.**
Gor. 1/9—20/10/56.**G.**
Rebuilt to Part 8.
Gor. 19/8—4/10/58.**C/L.**
Gor. 19/11—17/12/60.**H/I.**
Water treatment fitted.
Gor. 3/2—10/3/62.**C/L.**

BOILERS:
1097.
1440 7/3/31.
868 18/11/33.
518 12/10/35.
1174 21/8/37.
3291 14/10/39.
549 31/1/42.
3222 20/11/43.
3338 11/5/46.
3406 19/6/48.
22124 4/11/50.
22133 25/4/53.
28922 *(new)* 20/10/56.

SHEDS:
New England 24/7/28.
Grantham 7/11/28.
New England 19/1/31.
Colwick 14/5/31.
Langwith Jct. 18/5/31.
Tuxford 10/7/39.
Ardsley 27/9/53.

RENUMBERED:
6634 21/7/28.
3885 11/5/46.
63885 19/6/48.

CONDEMNED: 8/8/62.
Into Gor. for cut up 18/8/62.

6635

N.B. Loco. 22223 9/1919.

M of M 2133.

To traffic 25/9/28.

REPAIRS:
Gor. 23/6—22/9/28.**G.**
Gor. 22/8—19/9/31.**G.**
Gor. 9—23/12/33.**G.**
Gor. 7—21/3/36.**G.**
Intensifore removed.
Gor. 17—31/12/38.**G.**
Gor. 29/7—9/8/41.**G.**
Gor. 4—18/3/44.**G.**
Gor. 13/4/46.
Rebuilt to Class O1.

BOILERS:
929.
512 19/9/31.
1873 23/12/33.
3234 21/3/36.
1367 31/12/38.
1259 9/8/41.
1065 18/3/44.

SHEDS:
New England 25/9/28.
Boston 2/7/29.
New England 21/8/29.
Colwick 18/12/35.
Grantham 28/12/35.
Mexborough 21/11/42.
Woodford 7/9/44.

RENUMBERED:
6635 22/9/28.

6636

N.B. Loco. 22224 9/1919.

M of M 2134.

To traffic 2/8/27.

REPAIRS:
Gor. 2/7—2/8/27.**G.**
Gor. 2/7—20/8/29.**G.**
Gor. 25/5—16/7/31.**G.**
Gor. 14/8—7/10/33.**G.**
Gor. 16/7—11/8/34.**G.**
Gor. 24/9—31/10/36.**G.**
Intensifore removed.
Gor. 2/12/38—28/1/39.**G.**
Gor. 22/6—27/7/40.**G.**
Gor. 22/3—2/5/42.**G.**
Gor. 27/6—22/7/44.**G.**
Gor. 8/11/45.
Rebuilt to Class O1.

BOILERS:
1142.
1416 20/8/29.
1023 16/7/31.
1154 7/10/33.
1365 11/8/34.
1207 31/10/36.
1252 28/1/39.
3407 27/7/40.
1095 2/5/42.
1266 22/7/44.

SHEDS:
Doncaster 2/8/27.
Mexborough 23/11/36.
Langwith Jct. 11/5/37.
Frodingham 12/3/39.

RENUMBERED:
6636 2/8/27.

6637

N.B. Loco. 22225 9/1919.

M of M 2135.

To traffic 22/4/27.

REPAIRS:
Gor. 12/2—23/4/27.**G.**
Gor. 6/7—3/8/29.**G.**
Gor. 27/6—25/7/31.**G.**
Gor. 23—30/9/33.**G.**
Gor. 28/12/35—18/1/36.**G.**
Intensifore removed.
Fountain lub. to axles.
Gor. 9—23/7/38.**G.**
Gor. 14—21/12/40.**G.**
Gor. 4—15/5/43.**G.**
Gor. 20/10—3/11/45.**G.**
Gor. 26/12/47—5/2/48.**G.**
Gor. 17/6—1/7/50.**G.**
Gor. 4—15/7/50.**N/C.**
Gor. 6—20/12/52.**G.**
Gor. 23—30/12/52.**N/C.**
Gor. 19/11—24/12/55.**G.**
Gor. 31/3/60. *Not repaired.*

BOILERS:
1008.
1154 25/7/31.
1169 30/9/33.
1049 18/1/36.
3337 23/7/38.
3415 21/12/40.
3422 3/11/45.
1070 5/2/48.
3387 1/7/50.
22110 20/12/52.
22192 24/12/55.

SHEDS:
Gorton 22/4/27.

Brunswick 3/11/33.
Gorton 29/11/35.
Ardsley 25/11/45.
Mexborough 18/8/46.
Darnall 27/4/47.

RENUMBERED:
6637 23/4/27.
3888 2/11/46.
ᴇ3888 5/2/48.
63888 1/7/50.

CONDEMNED: 1/4/60.
Cut up at Gorton.

6638

N.B. Loco. 22226 9/1919.

M of M 2136.

To traffic 12/5/27.

REPAIRS:
Gor. 26/2—14/5/27.**G.**
Gor. 15/6—13/7/29.**G.**
Gor. 9—16/4/32.**G.**
Gor. 19/10—2/11/35.**G.**
Intensifore removed.
Gor. 27/11—4/12/37.**G.**
Gor. 6—13/7/40.**G.**
Str. 6/10—13/11/42.**G.**
Gor. 25—27/11/43.**L.**
Gor. 12—26/1/46.**G.**
Gor. 10—31/1/48.**G.**
Gor. 2—16/9/50.**G.**
Gor. 13/12/52—10/1/53.**G.**
Gor. 12—15/1/53.**N/C.**
Gor. 19—26/12/53.**C/L.**
After collision.
Gor. 19/11—17/12/55.**G.**
Gor. 8/6—6/7/57.**C/L.**
Gor. 11—12/7/57.**N/C.**
Gor. 17/11/59. *Not repaired.*

BOILERS:
1013.
1141 16/4/32.
1288 2/11/35.
3218 4/12/37.
3328 13/7/40.
1882 13/11/42.
3283 27/11/43.
3315 26/1/46.
3398 31/1/48.
22107 16/9/50.
22890 10/1/53.
22296 17/12/55.

SHEDS:
Cambridge 12/5/27.
Langwith Jct. 4/6/27.
Sheffield 7/9/29.
Staveley 23/1/34.

6638 continued/.
Darnall 6/2/49.

RENUMBERED:
6638 14/5/27.
3889 7/7/46.
E3889 31/1/48.
63889 16/9/50.

CONDEMNED: 2/12/59.
Cut up at Gorton.

___

6639

N.B. Loco. 22234 5/1919.

M of M 2144.

To traffic 9/11/27.

REPAIRS:
Gor. 22/10—9/11/27.**G.**
Gor. 28/12/29—4/1/30.**G.**
Gor. 3—?/8/32.**G.**
Gor. 2—?/4/35.**G.**
Gor. ?/?—28/8/37.**G.**
Gor. ?/?—?/1/40.**G.**
Gor. 28/7—22/8/42.**G.**
Gor. 23/7—12/8/44.**G.**
Gor. 16/3/46.
Rebuilt to Class O1.

BOILERS:
1221.
1211 ?/8/32.
1756 ?/4/35.
1147 28/8/37.
  42 ?/1/40.
1414 22/8/42.
3205 12/8/44.

SHEDS:
Immingham 9/11/27.
GWR. 22/11/40.
Woodford 20/7/42.
Staveley 3/4/44.

RENUMBERED:
6639 9/11/27.

___

6640

N.B. Loco. 22250 10/1919.

M of M 2160.

To traffic 16/6/27.

REPAIRS:
Gor. 30/4—16/6/27.**G.**
Gor. 20/6—25/7/29.**G.**
Gor. 31/1—24/3/31.**G.**
Gor. 7/5—17/6/33.**G.**

Gor. 23/9—7/11/35.**G.**
Intensifore removed.
Gor. 21/10—13/11/37.**G.**
Chimney altered.
Gor. 26/5—29/6/40.**G.**
Str.   11/10/42—18/2/43.**G.**
Gor. 28/1—3/3/45.**G.**
Gor. 7/4—18/5/47.**G.**
Gor. 20/10—4/12/48.**G.**
Gor. 28/11—24/12/49.**C/L.**
Gor. 29—30/12/49.**N/C.**
Gor. 1—20/1/51.**G.**
Gor. 10—29/11/52.**G.**
Gor. 29/6—5/9/55.**G.**
Rebuilt to Part 8.
Gor. 4—23/11/57.**C/L.**
Gor. 16/6—9/8/58.**G.**
Gor. 18—30/8/58.**N/C.**
Gor. 26/9—4/11/61.**H/I.**

BOILERS:
1077.
1457 24/3/31.
  42 17/6/33.
3218 7/11/35.
1275 13/11/37.
1464 29/6/40.
3257 3/3/45.
3385 18/5/47.
1232 4/12/48.
22110 20/1/51.
22118 29/11/52.
28392 *(ex63738)* 5/9/55.
28885 *(ex63651)* 9/8/58.

SHEDS:
Woodford 16/6/27.
Staveley 7/5/44.
Annesley 12/10/47.
Colwick 1/2/48.
Annesley 6/6/48.
Colwick 5/2/50.
Gorton 21/5/50.
Colwick 21/6/53.
Staveley 29/11/53.

RENUMBERED:
6640 16/6/27.
3899 7/7/46.
63899 4/12/48.

CONDEMNED: 25/5/63.
Into Don. for cut up 29/5/63.

___

6641

N.B. Loco. 22252 11/1919.

M of M 2162.

To traffic 18/8/27.

REPAIRS:
Gor. 21/5—20/8/27.**G.**

Gor. 26/4—24/5/30.**G.**
Gor. 17/10—7/11/31.**G.**
Gor. 31/3—14/4/34.**G.**
Gor. 29/8—19/9/36.**G.**
Intensifore removed.
Gor. 4—11/3/39.**G.**
Gor. 24/5—7/6/41.**G.**
Gor. 19—31/7/43.**G.**
Gor. 25/8—8/9/45.**G.**
Gor. 16/8—6/9/47.**G.**
Gor. 11—25/2/50.**G.**
Gor. 12—26/4/52.**G.**
Gor. 29—30/4/52.**N/C.**
Gor. 9/10—6/11/54.**G.**
Gor. 1—15/9/56.**C/L.**
Gor. 19—22/9/56.**N/C.**
Gor. 26/4—24/5/58.**G.**
Gor. 3—8/8/59.**N/C.**
Water treatment fitted.

BOILERS:
1148.
1030 24/5/30.
1353 7/11/31.
  820 14/4/34.
  803 19/9/36.
3362 11/3/39.
3241 7/6/41.
3248 31/7/43.
3402 8/9/45.
3387 6/9/47.
3226 25/2/50.
22119 26/4/52.
22236 6/11/54.
22262 24/5/58.

SHEDS:
Woodford 18/8/27.
Doncaster 28/9/28.
Woodford 4/12/28.
Staveley 19/6/37.
Woodford 7/5/44.
Langwith Jct. 7/4/46.
Doncaster 27/10/46.
Langwith Jct. 25/6/50.
Immingham 2/12/51.
Colwick 10/4/60.

RENUMBERED:
6641 20/8/27.
3900 18/8/46.
63900 25/2/50.

CONDEMNED: 23/9/62.
Sold for scrap to Round Oak Steel, Brierley Hill, 4/64.

___

6642

N.B. Loco. 22255 12/1919.

M of M 2165.

To traffic 7/6/27.

REPAIRS:
Gor. 19/3—11/6/27.**G.**
Gor. 2/11—7/12/29.**G.**
Gor. 3—24/10/31.**G.**
Gor. 14—21/10/33.**G.**
Gor. 18/1—1/2/36.**G.**
Intensifore removed.
Fountain lub. to axles.
Gor. 7—21/5/38.**G.**
Chimney altered.
Gor. 31/8—7/9/40.**G.**
Gor. 12—26/6/43.**G.**
Gor. 4/8/45.
Rebuilt to Class O1.

BOILERS:
1066.
1960 24/10/31.
1279 21/10/33.
C1474 1/2/36.
1458 21/5/38.
3335 7/9/40.
1231 26/6/43.

SHEDS:
Woodford 7/6/27.
Doncaster 25/9/28.
Woodford 28/11/28.
Immingham 20/2/30.
Tuxford 24/2/30.
Frodingham 30/11/33.

RENUMBERED:
6642 11/6/27.

___

O4/8. **No.63674 was withdrawn on 15th January 1966 from Colwick shed and in March was sold to contractors for cutting up. This 16th April 1966 photograph shows it at Cohen's scrap yard at Kettering. Note 1961-type high front on tender.**

(right) O4/8. **The last modification on Part 8 was to the tender when a high front plate with spectacle glasses and left hand end shaped for taking fire irons was put on. Its purpose was to provide protection when engines from Colwick shed worked iron ore trains tender first off the High Dyke branch. Four were fitted: 63816 (26th January), 63674 (11th March), 63675 (19th May), all 1961, and 63754 (16th February 1962).**

(below) O/4/8. **Although 63633 had a general repair, out on 19th August 1961, dieselization caused its withdrawal on 8th August 1962. Shown here on 19th August 1962 at Ardsley shed it was awaiting its call to Gorton for scrapping.**

The O5 class was completed by Gorton building Nos.14, 15, 17, 19 and 22 from November 1920 to February 1921 and on these five, a double side window cab with a rear extension piece to the roof was provided. No.17 was the only one of this batch to have crescent shape balance weights, the other four together with No.13 being built with the larger battleaxe shape. In July 1922, Nos.412 and 413 were changed from 5ft 6in. to 5ft 0in. boilers to provide two spare larger ones for interchanging.

Ex works 31st January 1920, No.420 was equipped for burning colloidal fuel, i.e. a mixture of oil and coal dust. The only external evidence was the oil tank on the tender which was carried until it went to works on 25th August 1923 after running 38,725 miles. No other engine was so fitted. Manchester London Road station, c1922.

CLASS O 5

5412

Gorton.

To traffic 1/1918.

REPAIRS:
Gor. 13/5/22.
Rebuilt to Class O4.

5413

Gorton.

To traffic 3/1918.

REPAIRS:
Gor. 29/4/22.
Rebuilt to Class O4.

5414

Gorton.

To traffic 4/1918.

REPAIRS:
Gor. 5/2—19/3/21.**G.**
Gor. 15/9—24/11/23.**G.**
Gor. 13/3—22/5/26.**G.**
Gor. 10/3—21/4/28.**G.**
Gor. 2—30/8/30.**G.**
Gor. 27/8—17/9/32.**G.**
Gor. 29/9—20/10/34.**G.**
Intensifore removed.
Gor. 24/10—14/11/36.**G.**
Rebuilt to O4/6 & heating apparatus removed.
Gor. 11/2—4/3/39.**G.**
Gor. 15/2—1/3/41.**G.**
Gor. 27/10—1/11/41.**L.**
Dragbox altered for Whitemoor hump.
Gor. 19/8—4/9/43.**G.**
Gor. 12/5—2/6/45.**H.**
Gor. 22/8—29/9/45.**L.**
Gor. 27/12/47—31/1/48.**G.**
Gor. 22/10—5/11/49.**C/L.**
After collision.
Gor. 2—23/6/51.**G.**
Gor. 26/6—1/7/51.**N/C.**
Gor. 3/7—21/8/54.**H/I.**
Gor. 9—30/3/57.**C/H.**
Gor. 5—26/4/58.**L/I.**
Gor. 29/4—6/5/58.**N/C.**
Gor. 15/11/61. *Not repaired.*

BOILERS:
1725.

1735 *(ex5415)* 22/5/26.
1739 *(ex5010)* 30/8/30.
1734 *(ex5421)* 17/9/32.
547 14/11/36.
1236 4/3/39.
3210 1/3/41.
1344 4/9/43.
1291 2/6/45.
927 31/1/48.
22193 23/6/51.
22270 30/3/57.

SHEDS:
Retford 5/8/21.
March 2/11/41.
Cambridge 22/12/47.
Mexborough 22/5/49.
Barnsley 21/8/49.
Mexborough 3/1/60.
Retford 9/7/61.

RENUMBERED:
5414 22/5/26.
3904 11/8/46.
ᴇ3904 31/1/48.
63904 5/11/49.

CONDEMNED: 23/11/61.
Cut up at Gorton.

5415

Gorton.

To traffic 5/1918.

REPAIRS:
Gor. 22/1—12/3/21.**G.**
Gor. 30/6—29/9/23.**G.**
Gor. 11/7—19/12/25.**G.**
Gor. 28/4—2/6/28.**G.**
Gor. 4/10—1/11/30.**G.**
Gor. 22/10—19/11/32.**G.**
Gor. 28/7—4/8/34.**G.**
Gor. 19/9—10/10/36.**G.**
Rebuilt to O4/6.
Intensifore removed.
Gor. 10—31/12/38.**G.**
Fountain lub. to axles.
Gor. 28/12/40—11/1/41.**G.**
Gor. 17/2—6/3/43.**G.**
Gor. 5/5—2/6/45.**G.**
Gor. 14/6—5/7/47.**G.**
Gor. 10—24/9/49.**G.**
Gor. 23/2—8/3/52.**G.**
Gor. 11—13/3/52.**N/C.**
Gor. 13—27/2/54.**G.**
Gor. 2—19/3/54.**N/C.**
Gor. 4/8—1/9/56.**G.**
Gor. 1/4/59. *Not repaired.*

BOILERS:
1726.
1735 *(ex5417)* 29/9/23.
1789 *(ex5010)* 19/12/25.
1719 *(ex5015)* 1/11/30.
1792 *(ex5422)* 4/8/34.
1059 10/10/36.
1947 31/12/38.
1102 11/1/41.
3225 6/3/43.
1858 2/6/45.
3366 5/7/47.
807 24/9/49.
22249 8/3/52.
22217 27/2/54.
22211 1/9/56.

SHED:
Retford 5/8/21.

RENUMBERED:
5415 19/12/25.
3905 1/4/46.
63905 24/9/49.

CONDEMNED: 8/4/59.
Cut up at Gorton.

5417

Gorton.

To traffic 6/1918.

REPAIRS:
Gor. 12/3—25/7/21.**G.**
Gor. 26/5—30/7/23.**G.**
Gor. 22/8/25—21/1/26.**G.**
Gor. 10/11/27—10/1/28.**G.**
Gor. 21/2—11/4/29.**G.**
Gor. 18/7—25/8/31.**G.**
Gor. 25/4—31/5/34.**G.**
Gor. 17/1—20/2/37.**G.**
Rebuilt to O4/6.
Intensifore & heating apparatus removed.
Gor. 6/4—4/5/40.**G.**
Gor. 24/2—17/4/43.**G.**
Gor. 14/8—29/9/45.**G.**
Gor. 25/1—21/2/48.**G.**
Gor. 8/6—29/7/50.**G.**
Gor. 7—30/8/52.**G.**
Gor. 15/12/54—12/2/55.**G.**
Gor. 21/9—16/11/57.**G.**
Gor. 4—26/6/59.**C/L.**
Gor. 18/4—18/5/61.**G.**

BOILERS:
1735.
1790 *(ex5011)* 30/7/23.

1788 *(ex5421)* 21/1/26.
11 *(ex5019)* 11/4/29.
1791 *(ex5422)* 25/8/31.
13 *(ex5010)* 31/5/34.
1267 *(ex5419)* 20/2/37.
3395 4/5/40.
825 17/4/43.
3334 29/9/45.
3403 21/2/48.
1118 *(ex63912)* 29/7/50.
22289 30/8/52.
22298 12/2/55.
22224 16/11/57.
22264 18/5/61.

SHEDS:
Mexborough 20/9/19.
Frodingham 25/12/49.

RENUMBERED:
5417 21/1/26.
3906 28/10/46.
ᴇ3906 21/2/48.
63906 29/7/50.

CONDEMNED: 3/1/65.
Sold for scrap to A.Draper, Hull, 2/65. Cut up 5/4/65.

5418

Gorton.

To traffic 8/1918.

REPAIRS:
Gor. 9/4—3/8/21.**G.**
Gor. 24/11/23—14/2/24.**G.**
Gor. 19/7—12/10/26.**G.**
Gor. 7/1—7/3/29.**G.**
Gor. 30/4—25/6/31.**G.**
Gor. 7/7—16/9/33.**G.**
Gor. 13/12/35—30/1/36.**G.**
Rebuilt to O4/6.
Intensifore removed.
Gor. 6/2—5/3/38.**G.**
Gor. 10/3—6/4/40.**G.**
Gor. 5/6—4/7/42.**G.**
Gor. 5/2—24/4/43.**L.**
Gor. 23/10—18/11/44.**G.**
Gor. 13/5—12/6/46.**G.**
Gor. 23/5—23/6/48.**G.**
Gor. 5/6—22/7/50.**G.**
Gor. 3—22/11/52.**G.**
Gor. 9/2—17/3/56.**G.**
Gor. 5/2—11/3/60.**H/I.**

BOILERS:
1736.
1724 14/2/24.

183

When No.422 was new in June 1919 it was fitted to burn pulverised fuel, carried by this large double bogie tender. By Grouping this tender had moved to No.966 and 422 had a standard 4000 gallons type.

(*above*) **Ex works on 7th February 1925 as No.5422, the engine still had top feed, Robinson circulator, blower and Intensifore lubrication. No change had then been made to the footsteps, piston tail rods, or to the chimney, but oval headed buffers had been substituted. Mexborough shed, 13th April 1925.**

(*left*) **By its June 1931 repair, No.5422 had lost the top feed, tail rods, and the footsteps half way along the running plate. The combined circulating and blower arrangement had been removed, but no other protection for superheater elements was in evidence.**

5418 continued.
1789 *(ex5415)* 25/6/31.
1308 30/1/36.
1168 5/3/38.
1314 6/4/40.
3287 4/7/42.
3389 18/11/44.
1129 12/6/46.
3394 23/6/48.
3277 22/7/50.
22878 22/11/52.
22139 17/3/56.

SHEDS:
Retford 5/8/21.
Barnsley 18/3/51.
Mexborough 3/1/60.
Langwith Jct. 1/3/64.

RENUMBERED:
5418 14/2/24.
3907 31/3/46.
63907 19/6/48.

CONDEMNED: 22/5/64.
Sold for scrap to Cox & Danks,
Wadsley Bridge, 8/64.

_____

5419

Gorton.

To traffic 9/1918.

REPAIRS:
Gor. 4/6—7/8/21.**G**.
Gor. 3/11/23—16/1/24.**G**.
Gor. 19/7—23/10/26.**G**.
Gor. 8/1—15/2/29.**G**.
Gor. 1/11—19/12/30.**G**.
Gor. 7/1—14/2/31.**G**.
Gor. 5/1—10/3/33.**G**.
Gor. 28/2—6/4/35.**G**.
Rebuilt to O4/6.
Intensifore removed.
Gor. 28/12/36—30/1/37.**G**.
Gor. 8/4—20/5/39.**G**.
Gor. 8/6—19/7/41.**G**.
Gor. 14/12/42—16/1/43.**G**.
Gor. 13/8—6/10/45.**G**.
Gor. 2/2—7/7/47.**L**.
Gor. 4/9—31/10/47.**G**.
Gor. 20/11—17/12/49.**G**.
Gor. 20—26/12/49.**G**.
Gor. 2/2—1/3/52.**G**.
Gor. 4—5/3/52.**N/C**.
Gor. 1—30/4/54.**G**.
Gor. 3—7/5/54.**N/C**.
Gor. 10/12/57—1/3/58.**G**.
Gor. 16—19/4/58.**N/C**.

BOILERS:
1737.
1738 *(ex5420)* 16/1/24.
 13 *(ex5014)* 15/2/29.
1735 *(ex5414)* 19/12/30.
1737 *(ex5022)* 10/3/33.
1267 6/4/35.
1070 30/1/37.
1259 20/5/39.
3244 19/7/41.
3422 16/1/43.
1239 6/10/45.
 804 *(ex3730)* 31/10/47.
1237 17/12/49.
22248 1/3/52.
22215 30/4/54.
22249 1/3/58.

SHEDS:
Retford 24/3/22.
Langwith Jct. 10/9/50.
Immingham 2/12/51.
Colwick 20/9/53.
Mexborough 29/1/56.
Retford 26/11/61.

RENUMBERED:
5419 23/10/26.
3908 24/11/46.
63908 17/12/49.

CONDEMNED: 1/10/63.
Sold for scrap to ??, 1/64.

_____

5420

Gorton.

To traffic 4/1919.

REPAIRS:
Gor. 3—31/1/20.**L**.
Adapted to burn fuel oil.
Gor. 25/8—13/10/23.**G**.
Gor. 10/4—21/8/26.**G**.
Gor. 16/7—3/9/27.**G**.
Gor. 18/5—8/6/29.**G**.
Gor. 28/11—12/12/31.**G**.
Cambridge shed. 4/32.
Drag box altered to obviate
breaking on Whitemoor hump.
Gor. 25/2—18/3/33.**L**.
Rail washing gear fitted.
Gor. 14/9—5/10/35.**G**.
Intensifore removed.
Gor. 1—22/10/38.**G**.
Number still on tender when
entering works.
Gor. 1—13/9/41.**G**.
Rebuilt to O4/6.

BOILERS:
1738.
1726 *(ex5415)* 13/10/23.
1790 *(ex5417)* 21/8/26.
1788 *(ex5417)* 8/6/29.
1738 *(ex5419)* 12/12/31.
 64 *(exB6 5052)* 5/10/35.
1726 *(exB6 5416)* 22/10/38.
3439 13/9/41.

SHEDS:
Gorton 12/3/20.
Mexborough 9/2/24.
March 28/3/32.

RENUMBERED:
5420 21/8/26.

WITHDRAWN: 14/9/41.
Reno.733 and sent to Middle
East via Greenock, 9/10/41.

_____

5421

Gorton.

To traffic 7/1919.

REPAIRS:
Gor. 16/10—11/12/20.**G**.
Gor. 9/12/22—17/2/23.**G**.
Gor. 6/9—1/11/24.**G**.
Gor. 25/4—9/5/25.**L**.
Gor. 29/10—3/12/27.**G**.
Gor. 23/2—30/3/29.**G**.
Gor. 10—31/10/31.**G**.
Cambridge shed. 4/32.
Drag box altered to obviate
breaking on Whitemoor hump.
Gor. 20—27/5/33.**L**.
Rail washing gear fitted.
Gor. 5—19/10/35.**G**.
Intensifore & heating apparatus
removed.
Gor. 3/9—1/10/38.**G**.
Gor. 23/9—11/10/41.**G**.
Rebuilt to O4/6.

BOILERS:
1788.
1736 *(ex5418)* 1/11/24.
1734 *(exB6 5416)* 3/12/27.
 1 *(ex5013)* 31/10/31.
1738 *(ex5420)* 19/10/35.
 58 *(ex5013)* 1/10/38.
3421 11/10/41.

SHEDS:
Mexborough 20/9/19.
March 1/4/32.

RENUMBERED:
5421 1/11/24.

WITHDRAWN: 11/10/41.
Reno.781 and sent to Mid. East.

_____

5422

Gorton.

To traffic 6/1919. *Fitted with*
pulveriser.

REPAIRS:
Gor. 28/8—4/9/20.**L**.
Gor. 20/1—10/3/23.**G**.
Pulveriser removed.
Gor. 6/12/24—7/2/25.**G**.
Gor. 20/8—8/10/27.**G**.
Gor. 16/3—20/4/29.**G**.
Gor. 6—27/6/31.**G**.
Gor. 9—23/6/34.**G**.
Gor. 20/2—6/3/37.**G**.
Intensifore removed.
Gor. 23/12/39—13/1/40.**G**.
Gor. 5—23/1/43.**G**.
Rebuilt to O4/6.
Gor. 10/2—3/3/45.**G**.
Gor. 28/6—9/8/47.**G**.
Gor. 19/11—10/12/49.**G**.
Gor. 16—30/12/50.**C/L**.
Gor. 3—4/1/51.**N/C**.
Gor. 26/4—24/5/52.**G**.
Gor. 27—28/5/52.**N/C**.
Gor. 25/9—23/10/54.**G**.
Gor. 7/12/57—11/1/58.**G**.
Gor. 5—12/4/58.**C/L**.
After collision.

BOILERS:
1739.
1791 *(ex5012)* 8/10/27.
1792 *(ex5010)* 27/6/31.
1791 *(ex5417)* 23/6/34.
 873 *(exB6 5052)* 6/3/37.
3275 *(new)* 23/1/43.
1190 *(ex5012)* 3/3/45.
3264 9/8/47.
3382 10/12/49.
3382 reno.22148 30/12/50.
22128 24/5/52.
22257 23/10/54.
22162 11/1/58.

SHEDS:
Gorton 28/6/19.
Mexborough 9/2/24.
Doncaster 18/8/46.
Frodingham 18/1/48.
Barnsley 13/11/55.

_____

WORKS CODES:- Bpk - Beyer, Peacock. Crw - Crewe. Cw - Cowlairs. Dar- Darlington. Dhy - Derby. Don - Doncaster. Ghd - Gateshead. Gor - Gorton. Inv - Inverurie. Str - Stratford.
REPAIR CODES:- C/H - Casual Heavy. C/L - Casual Light. G - General. H- Heavy. H/I - Heavy Intermediate. L - Light. L/I - Light Intermediate. N/C - Non-Classified.

(*above*) No.413 changed from this 5ft 6in. boiler when ex works on 1st July 1922, and from February 1924 to April 1931 the boiler was on No.5418, but was then condemned. Like No.412 it had tall Ross 'pop' safety valves however, without the base cover.

(*left*) After the LNER took over, the first change was the removal of the combined blower and circulating valve from the left-hand side of the smokebox. Although built with battleaxe balance weights, 5013 changed to the crescent shape, probably in 1923. Next to go was the top feed, from No.5013 almost certainly when ex works on 7th April 1928. Note Southern Area Load class 7 collar fitted on the vacuum standpipe.

(above) Even the short Robinson chimney needed replacement due to cracking and by 1932 a 'plantpot' type was being put on. Note that a Gresley type anti-vacuum valve had also been introduced.

(left) Another with 'plantpot' chimney was No.5011, so fitted ex works on 29th July 1933, but this September 1935 photograph shows it did not get an anti-vacuum valve because it went for re-boilering to O4/6 on 22nd March 1936. Annesley, 19th September 1935.

5422 continued.
Mexborough 3/1/60.

RENUMBERED:
5422 7/2/25.
3911 15/9/46.
63911 10/12/49.

CONDEMNED: 9/12/62.
Sold for scrap to Round Oak Steel, Brierly Hill, 3/64.

5010

Gorton.

To traffic 8/1919.

REPAIRS:
Gor. 22/1—5/3/21.**G**.
Gor. 10/2—14/4/23.**G**.
Gor. 17/1—28/2/25.**G**.
Gor. 1/10—5/11/27.**G**.
Gor. 12/10—2/11/29.**G**.
Gor. 31/1—21/2/31.**G**.
Gor. 16/8—16/9/33.**G**.
Gor. 23/5—13/6/36.**G**.
Intensifore removed.
Gor. 8/10—5/11/38.**G**.
Gor. 14—26/7/41.**G**.
Rebuilt to O4/6.
Gor. 4—18/12/43.**G**.
Gor. 14/9—12/10/46.**G**.
Gor. 19/2—5/3/49.**G**.
Gor. 7—21/4/51.**G**.
Gor. 23—27/4/51.**N/C**.
Gor. 29/11/52—10/1/53.**C/L**.
After collision.
Gor. 1—15/8/53.**G**.
Gor. 18—25/8/53.**N/C**.
Gor. 25/2—24/3/56.**G**.
Gor. 9/5—6/6/59.**G**.
Water treatment gear fitted.

BOILERS:
1789.
 5 (*ex5011*) 28/2/25.
1739 (*ex5422*) 5/11/27.
1792 (*ex5013*) 2/11/29.
 13 (*ex5419*) 21/2/31.
1736 (*ex5019*) 16/9/33.
 1 (*ex5421*) 13/6/36.
 64 (*ex5420*) 5/11/38.
3325 26/7/41.
1023 18/12/43.
3274 12/10/46.
3413 5/3/49.
22178 21/4/51.
22137 15/8/53.
22893 24/3/56.
22110 6/6/59.

SHEDS:
Mexborough 17/10/19.

Colwick 18/9/44.
Staveley 30/9/44.
Annesley 12/10/47.
Gorton 26/11/50.
Colwick 4/5/52.
Darnall 18/7/54.
Tuxford 9/1/55.
Langwith Jct. 1/2/59.

RENUMBERED:
5010 28/2/25.
3912 26/5/46.
63912 5/3/49.

CONDEMNED: 9/12/62.
Sold for scrap to J.Cashmore, Great Bridge, 5/63.

5011

Gorton.

To traffic 8/1919.

REPAIRS:
Gor. 29/1—9/4/21.**G**.
Gor. 5/5—13/7/23.**G**.
Gor. 19/9—21/11/24.**G**.
Gor. 19/8—15/10/27.**G**.
Gor. 25/1—12/3/29.**G**.
Gor. 28/8—9/10/31.**G**.
Gor. 26/4—29/7/33.**G**.
Gor. 22/3—1/5/36.**G**.
Rebuilt to O4/6.Intensifore & heating apparatus removed.
Gor. 24/5—16/7/38.**G**.
Gor. 27/2—15/3/41.**G**.
Gor. 27/9—23/10/43.**G**.
Gor. 23/7—6/10/45.**G**.
Gor. 31/12/47—18/2/48.**G**.
Gor. 1—3/3/48.**N/C**.
Gor. 3—28/10/50.**G**.
Gor. 1—3/11/50.**N/C**.
Gor. 20/8—12/9/53.**G**.
Gor. 12/11—29/12/56.**G**.
Gor. 20/6—26/8/61.**G**.
Gor. 1—9/9/61.**N/C**.

BOILERS:
1790.
 5 (*ex5017*) 13/7/23.
1737 (*ex5419*) 21/11/24.
1726 (*ex5420*) 15/10/27.
 11 (*ex5417*) 9/10/31.
1081 1/5/36.
 943 16/7/38.
3245 15/3/41.
1281 23/10/43.
3404 6/10/45.
3424 18/2/48.
22122 28/10/50.
22178 12/9/53.
22233 29/12/56.
22228 26/8/61.

SHEDS:
Mexborough 15/11/19.
Langwith Jct. 7/6/37.
Barnsley 21/6/39.
March 2/11/41.
Cambridge 22/12/47.
Mexborough 22/5/49.
Barnsley 21/8/49.
Mexborough 3/1/60.
Staveley 11/2/62.

RENUMBERED:
5011 21/11/24.
3913 11/8/46.
ᴇ3913 18/2/48.
63913 28/10/50.

CONDEMNED: 6/6/65.
Sold for scrap to Cox & Danks, Wadsley Bridge, 7/65.

5012

Gorton.

To traffic 9/1919.

REPAIRS:
Gor. 19/2—18/7/21.**G**.
Gor. 12/5—15/8/23.**G**.
Gor. 31/3—6/8/26.**G**.
Rebuilt to O4/6.
Gor. 22/6—21/8/28.**G**.
Gor. 18/10—4/12/30.**G**.
Gor. 1—27/10/34.**G**.
Gor. 27/7—14/8/37.**G**.
Intensifore removed.
Gor. 24/8—7/9/40.**G**.
Gor. 28/6—5/9/42.**G**.
Gor. 10/12/44—13/1/45.**G**.
Gor. 8/12/46—25/1/47.**G**.
Gor. 3/3—2/4/49.**G**.
Gor. 15/2—24/3/51.**G**.
Gor. 28/3—24/4/51.**N/C**.
Gor. 1—20/6/53.**G**.
Gor. 23/6—2/7/53.**N/C**.
Gor. 18/5—30/7/55.**G**.
Rebuilt to O4/8.
Gor. 9—10/8/55.**N/C**.
Gor. 8/5—7/6/58.**G**.
Gor. 18/3—22/4/61.**H/I**.

BOILERS:
1791.
1944 6/8/26.
1956 4/12/30.
1867 27/10/34.
1093 14/8/37.
3212 7/9/40.
1190 5/9/42.
3401 13/1/45.
3266 25/1/47.
3355 2/4/49.
22168 24/3/51.

22192 20/6/53.
28881 (*new*) 30/7/55.
28313 (*ex63639*) 7/6/58.

SHEDS:
Mexborough 12/12/19.
Retford 13/1/46.

RENUMBERED:
5012 6/8/26.
3914 13/10/46.
63914 2/4/49.

CONDEMNED: 28/5/64.
Sold for scrap to Bulwell Forest Wagon Works, 8/64.

5013

Gorton.

To traffic 10/1919.

REPAIRS:
Gor. 9/4—28/5/21.**G**.
Gor. 12/5—25/8/23.**G**.
Gor. 14/3—14/11/25.**G**.
Gor. 25/2—7/4/28.**G**.
Gor. 16/3—6/4/29.**G**.
Gor. 19/9—3/10/31.**G**.
Gor. 13/10—3/11/34.**G**.
Intensifore removed.
Gor. 19—26/6/37.**G**.
Heating apparatus removed.
Gor. 18/5—1/6/40.**G**.
Rebuilt to O4/6.
Gor. 15/5—12/6/43.**G**.
Gor. 22/12/45—12/1/46.**G**.
Gor. 10/4—1/5/48.**G**.
Gor. 18/2—4/3/50.**C/L**.
Gor. 4—18/8/51.**G**.
Gor. 21—24/8/51.**N/C**.
Gor. 29/8—19/9/53.**G**.
Gor. 7/11/53.**N/C**.
Gor. 22/10/55—7/1/56.**G**.
Rebuilt to O4/8.
Gor. 25/10—22/11/58.**G**.

BOILERS:
1792.
 1 (*ex5015*) 6/4/29.
 58 (*exB6 5052*) 3/10/31.
1791 (*ex5422*) 26/6/37.
3229 (*ex5022*) 1/6/40.
3350 12/6/43.
3313 12/1/46.
3204 1/5/48.
22208 18/8/51.
22210 19/9/53.
28887 (*new*) 7/1/56.
28359 (*exO1 63619*) 22/11/58.

SHEDS:
Mexborough 17/1/20.

Some of the original cast chimneys survived to be seen with anti-vacuum valve on the smokebox. Note the shorter type of Ross 'pop' safety valve. In the 1930's Intensifore lubrication was taken off and replaced by a Wakefield mechanical type. No.5013 was so changed when ex works on 3rd November 1934 and No.5422 to 20th February 1937 was the last O5 with Intensifore.

No.5417 got a 'plantpot' probably when ex works on 31st May 1934, but no protection for the superheater elements was put on. Note the extra sanding from boxes on the front end of the tender to assist the effect of its brakes.

Until 1927/28 two sets of footsteps were carried (*see* middle illustration, page 208) but those half way along the running plate were then dispensed with. The single step on the bar, linking the ends of the crosshead slides was then given a plate backing and an additional step. Doncaster shed, October 1931.

All the tenders were fitted with water pick-up apparatus, and whilst still O5 class, probably retained it.

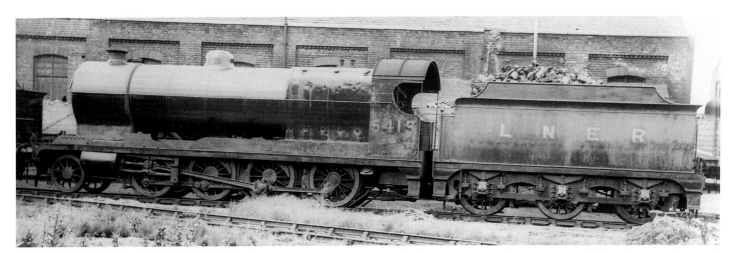

The first fourteen built had a normal GCR style cab with cut-out, and the roof had angle irons to give extra strength. The chimney, dome, and cab heights from rail all exceeded 13ft 0in. and no O5 was brought within the LNER 13ft 0in. load gauge. Retford, 3rd July 1932.

Only the last five, Nos.5014, 5015, 5017, 5019 and 5022 had the cab with two side windows and the rear roof extension. No others were changed to this style, nor were any fitted with hinged sightscreens on the cab side. Except for No.5017, this batch were built with battleaxe balance weights - Nos.5014, 5015, 5019 and 5022 retained them, but No.5013 exchanged wheels sets with No.5420, probably in 1923.

For their work on hump shunting at Whitemoor, Nos.5420 and 5421 had a light frame fitted on the tender, curved to the same profile as the cab roof, on which a tarpaulin could be connected to the roof (*see* bottom illustration). These two were also fitted with rail-washing gear in 1933, Nos.5420 (18th March) and 5421 (27th May). Note screw coupling, but *see* also final O5 illustration on page 217.

Although always painted black, at Grouping they had full GCR goods livery with a double lining panel on the cab side and on the tender.

Some of the original painting was so good that with occasional touching up, it lasted almost twenty years. Until it went to works on 1st October 1938, No.5420 still had its number on the tender and the GCR double lining on cab and tender was still readily discernible. March shed, 16th June 1935.

5013 continued.
Doncaster 18/8/46.
Gorton 21/5/50.
Immingham 17/8/52.
Langwith Jct. 20/9/53.
Gorton 8/1/56.

RENUMBERED:
5013 14/11/25.
3915 21/8/46.
63915 1/5/48.

CONDEMNED: 23/6/61.
Into Gor. for cut up 24/6/61.

———————————————

5014

Gorton.

To traffic 11/1920.

REPAIRS:
Gor. 7/4—9/6/23.**G.**
Gor. 16/5—18/7/25.**G.**
Gor. 19/5—23/6/28.**G.**
Gor. 19/4—31/5/30.**G.**
Gor. 24/12/32—21/1/33.**G.**
Rebuilt to O4/6.
Gor. 19/10—2/11/35.**G.**
Intensifore & heat app.removed.
Gor. 26/11—10/12/38.**G.**
Gor. 29/9—25/10/41.**G.**

BOILERS:
  1.
  13 (ex5022) 9/6/23.
  873 (new) 23/6/28.
1187 21/1/33.
1077 2/11/35.
1085 10/12/38.
3357 (ex5017) 25/10/41.

SHEDS:
Sheffield 11/2/21.
Mexborough 22/3/24.

RENUMBERED:
5014 18/7/25.

WITHDRAWN: 25/10/41.
Reno.787 and sent to Mid. East.

———————————————

5015

Gorton.

To traffic 12/1920.

REPAIRS:
Gor. 21/4—23/6/23.**G.**
Gor. 4/7—29/8/25.**G.**
Gor. 4/8—15/9/28.**G.**
Gor. 25/1—15/2/30.**G.**

Gor. 9—30/7/32.**G.**
Gor. 8—29/6/35.**G.**
Rebuilt to O4/6.
Intensifore removed.
Gor. 3—24/4/37.**G.**
Gor. 1—8/6/40.**G.**
Gor. 17/4—8/5/43.**G.**
Gor. 26/1—16/2/46.**G.**
Gor. 17/4—8/5/48.**G.**
Gor. 26/8—9/9/50.**G.**
Gor. 13—25/9/50.**N/C.**
Gor. 30/8—13/9/52.**G.**
Gor. 18/12/54—29/1/55.**G.**
Gor. 18/5—15/6/57.**G.**
Gor. 18—19/6/57.**N/C.**
Gor. 11/5—24/6/60.**H/I.**
Gor. 1—9/7/60.**N/C.**
Gor. 1/6/62. *Not repaired.*

BOILERS:
  2.
  1 (ex5014) 23/6/23.
1719 (ex5022) 15/9/28.
1790 (ex5420) 15/2/30.
1726 (ex5011) 30/7/32.
1968 29/6/35.
1271 24/4/37.
1118 8/6/40.
  815 8/5/43.
3253 16/2/46.
3209 8/5/48.
22103 9/9/50.
22294 13/9/52.
22253 29/1/55.
22261 15/6/57.

SHEDS:
Sheffield 11/2/21.
Mexborough 3/3/24.
Darnall 27/4/47.
Immingham 4/10/47.
Frodingham 10/12/49.

RENUMBERED:
5015 29/8/25.
3917 18/8/46.
63917 8/5/48.

CONDEMNED: 5/6/62.
Cut up at Gorton.

———————————————

5017

Gorton.

To traffic 12/1920.

REPAIRS:
Gor. 28/4—7/7/23.**G.**
Gor. 7/11—26/12/25.**G.**
Gor. 28/7—18/8/28.**G.**
Gor. 15/3—12/4/30.**G.**
Gor. 15—29/10/32.**G.**
Rebuilt to O4/6.

Gor. 26/10—9/11/35.**G.**
*Intensifore & heating apparatus
removed.*
Gor. 19/11—3/12/38.**G.**
Gor. 29/9—18/10/41.**G.**

BOILERS:
  5.
  2 (ex5015) 7/7/23.
  5 (ex5010) 18/8/28.
1221 29/10/32.
3217 (new) 9/11/35.
3357 3/12/38.
1961 18/10/41.

SHEDS:
Sheffield 4/3/21.
Mexborough 3/3/24.

RENUMBERED:
5017 26/12/25.

WITHDRAWN: 18/10/41.
Reno.766 and sent to Mid. East.

———————————————

5019

Gorton.

To traffic 1/1921.

REPAIRS:
Gor. 7/4—23/6/23.**G.**
Gor. 2/5—4/7/25.**G.**
Gor. 18/8—22/9/28.**G.**
Gor. 9/8—20/9/30.**G.**
Gor. 15/7—5/8/33.**G.**
Rebuilt to O4/6.
Gor. 18—25/7/36.**G.**
Intensifore removed.
Gor. 13—27/5/39.**G.**
Gor. 1—13/9/41.**G.**

BOILERS:
  11.
1736 (ex5421) 22/9/28.
1861 5/8/33.
3255 25/7/36.
3435 13/9/41.

SHEDS:
Sheffield 18/3/21.
Mexborough 3/3/24.
Frodingham 23/8/39.

RENUMBERED:
5019 4/7/25.

WITHDRAWN: 14/9/41.
*Reno.721 and sent to Middle
East via Hull 23/9/41.*

———————————————

5022

Gorton.

To traffic 2/1921.

REPAIRS:
Gor. 17/3—21/4/23.**G.**
Gor. 31/10—19/12/25.**G.**
Gor. 28/7—18/8/28.**G.**
Gor. 12/4—31/5/30.**G.**
Gor. 26/11—10/12/32.**G.**
Gor. 14/9—5/10/35.**G.**
*Rebuilt to O4/6. Intensifore &
heating apparatus removed.*
Gor. 24/12/37—8/1/38.**G.**
Gor. 20/4—4/5/40.**G.**
Gor. 1—13/6/42.**G.**
Gor. 8—29/7/44.**G.**
Gor. 2—23/11/46.**G.**
Gor. 2—23/4/49.**G.**
Gor. 1—15/9/51.**G.**
Gor. 18—22/9/51.**N/C.**
Gor. 27/2—20/3/54.**G.**
Gor. 23—26/3/54.**N/C.**
Gor. 1—29/12/56.**G.**
Gor. 18/3—22/4/61.**H/I.**
Water treatment fitted.

BOILERS:
  13.
1719 (new) 21/4/23.
1737 (ex5011) 18/8/28.
  5 (ex5017) 10/12/32.
1135 5/10/35.
3229 8/1/38.
3332 4/5/40.
1323 13/6/42.
  858 29/7/44.
3278 23/11/46.
3402 23/4/49.
22215 15/9/51.
22202 20/3/54.
22133 29/12/56.

SHEDS:
Sheffield 15/4/21.
Mexborough 22/3/24.
Langwith Jct. 9/6/37.
Doncaster 11/1/39.
Gorton 3/2/43.
Frodingham 6/12/44.
Ardsley 22/9/52.
Bradford 6/12/53.
Ardsley 5/1/58.
Wakefield 22/2/59.

RENUMBERED:
5022 19/12/25.
3920 22/9/46.
63920 23/4/49.

CONDEMNED: 8/8/62.
Into Gor. for cut up ?/10/62.

———————————————

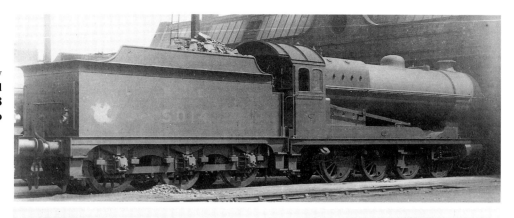

No.5014, ex works on 18th July 1925, had the LNER single red lining, used until the June 1928 painting economies put an end to it. Annesley shed, 6th June 1926.

Where repainting took place after March 1929, the number was moved to the cab (No.5418 from 25th June 1931) and the LNER on the tender became 12in. instead of 7½ in. high.

Not until it was ex works on 22nd October 1938 did No.5420 have its number moved to the cab side. Although built with crescent shape balance weights (*see* page 206, bottom), wheel sets with battleaxe shape weights were substituted, probably in 1923. March shed, 16th June 1935.

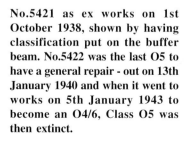

No.5421 as ex works on 1st October 1938, shown by having classification put on the buffer beam. No.5422 was the last O5 to have a general repair - out on 13th January 1940 and when it went to works on 5th January 1943 to become an O4/6, Class O5 was then extinct.

By the end of the LNER, fifty-one O4's had been rebuilt to O1, and seven more were done by British Railways, the last being No.63856, ex Gorton 22nd October 1949. The thirty-seven rebuilt in 1944/45 at first had only NE on the tender, but beginning with No.6216, ex works 19th January 1946, LNER was used again.

Fourteen of the rebuilds had originally been in Part 1 of Class O4. These were: Nos.5385, 5394, 5408, 6195, 6213, 6214, 6216, 6220, 6231, 6243, 6244, 6245, 3594 (ex 5333) and 63571 (ex 6224).

CLASS O 1

63571
(ex 6224/3571)

Gorton, rebuilt from O4/1.

To traffic 27/8/1949.

REPAIRS:
Gor. 22/9—13/10/51.**G**.
Gor. 27/9—18/10/52.**C/L**.
Gor. 29/8—12/9/53.**G**.
Gor. 9—23/10/54.**C/L**.
Gor. 30/7—3/9/55.**G**.
Gor. 17/8—14/9/57.**G**.
Don. 9/1—7/3/62.**G**.

BOILERS:
5119.
28353 *(ex63856)* 13/10/51.
28303 *(ex63773)* 12/9/53.
28883 *(new)* 3/9/55.
28286 *(ex63838)* 14/9/57.
28463 *(exB1 61367)* 7/3/62.

SHEDS:
Annesley 27/8/49.
March 3/3/57.
Staveley 3/1/60.

RENUMBERED:
63571 27/8/49.

CONDEMNED: 13/12/64.
Sold for scrap to A.Draper,
Hull, 2/65. Cut up 29/3/65.

6231

Gorton, rebuilt from O4/1.

To traffic 13/10/1945.

REPAIRS:
Gor. ?/?—?/2/46.**N/C**.
Drop grate fitted.
Gor. 8/11—14/12/47.**G**.
Gor. 2—28/1/50.**G**.
S/C smokebox fitted.
Gor. 31/1—2/2/50.**N/C**.
Gor. 29/4—9/6/51.**C/H**.
Gor. 23/1—14/2/53.**G**.
Gor. 5—27/2/54.**C/L**.
Gor. 29/12/54—4/2/55.**G**.
Gor. 22/2—17/3/56.**C/L**.
Gor. 22/2—20/4/57.**G**.
Gor. 8—23/8/58.**L**.
After collision.
Gor. 6/2—11/3/61.**H/I**.

BOILERS:
5044.
5113 *(new)* 14/12/47.
5043 *(ex3808)* 28/1/50.
5043 reno.28325 9/6/51.
28257 *(ex63652)* 14/2/53.
28387 *(ex63872)* 4/2/55.
28901 *(ex63594)* 20/4/57.

SHEDS:
Colwick 13/10/45.
Gorton 21/10/45.
Annesley 16/7/50.

RENUMBERED:
3578 27/11/46.
63578 28/1/50.

CONDEMNED: 17/11/62.
Into Dby. for cut up 6/63.

ᴇ3579
(ex 6232/3579)

Gorton, rebuilt from O4/5.

To traffic 13/3/1948.

REPAIRS:
Gor. 30/11—31/12/49.**G**.
Gor. 3—16/1/50.**N/C**.
Gor. 8/1—2/2/52.**G**.
Gor. 2—28/2/53.**C/L**.
Gor. 2—21/11/53.**G**.
Gor. 17/3—10/4/54.**C/L**.
Gor. 5/10—20/11/54.**C/L**.
Gor. 14/12/55—26/1/56.**G**.
Gor. 3/2—8/3/58.**G**.
Gor. 19—22/3/58.**N/C**.
Gor. 17/11—15/12/59.**C/L**.
Gor. 23/6—23/8/62.**G**.

BOILERS:
5100.
5010 *(ex3879)* 31/12/49.
28825 *(new)* 2/2/52.
28339 *(ex63760)* 21/11/53.
28889 *(new)* 26/1/56.
28813 *(exO4/8 63706)* 23/8/62.

SHEDS:
Darnall 13/3/48.
Annesley 16/1/49.
March 24/2/57.
Annesley 14/4/57.

RENUMBERED:
ᴇ3579 13/3/48.
63579 27/3/48.

CONDEMNED: 21/11/62.
Into Crw. for cut up 9/63.

63589
(ex 6242/3589)

Gorton, rebuilt from O4/5.

To traffic 28/4/1949.

REPAIRS:
Gor. 12/11/50—9/2/51.**G**.
Gor. 7—21/2/53.**G**.
Gor. 15/1—5/2/55.**G**.
Gor. 26/1—16/2/57.**G**.
Gor. 16/11—12/12/59.**G**.
Don. 28/9—30/11/62.**G**.

BOILERS:
5109.
28289 *(ex63890)* 9/2/51.
28840 *(new)* 21/2/53.
28391 *(ex63817)* 5/2/55.
28855 *(ex63768)* 16/2/57.
28811 *(ex63591)* 12/12/59.
28957 *(ex63929)* 30/11/62.

SHEDS:
Annesley 30/4/49.
Colwick 3/11/57.
Staveley 9/6/63.
Langwith Jct. 13/6/65.

RENUMBERED:
63589 28/4/49.

CONDEMNED: 11/7/65.
Sold for scrap to A.Draper,
Hull. Cut up 25/10/65.

6243

Gorton, rebuilt from O4/1.

To traffic 16/12/1944.

REPAIRS:
Gor. 8/2—22/3/47.**G**.
Gor. 4/6—1/7/49.**G**.
Gor. 20/3—22/4/50.**C/L**.
Gor. 16/10—16/12/50.**C/L**.
Gor. 10/4—26/5/51.**C/H**.
Gor. 17—24/11/51.**C/L**.
Gor. 18/4—17/5/52.**G**.
Gor. 16/2—18/3/54.**G**.
Gor. 22/2—2/4/55.**C/L**.
Gor. 6/3—14/4/56.**G**.
Gor. 6/8—13/9/58.**G**.

Gor. 10/2—16/3/60.**C/L**.
Don. 9/7—20/9/62.**G**.

BOILERS:
5014.
5036 *(ex3817)* 22/3/47.
5030 *(ex3619)* 1/7/49.
5030 reno.28274 16/12/50.
28832 *(new)* 17/5/52.
28363 *(ex63725)* 18/3/54.
28314 *(ex63610)* 14/4/56.
28379 *(ex63646)* 13/9/58.

SHEDS:
Frodingham 16/12/44.
Gorton 7/1/45.
Colwick 18/8/46.
Gorton 20/10/46.
Annesley 26/11/50.
March 3/3/57.
Staveley 15/11/59.
Langwith Jct. 13/6/65.

RENUMBERED:
3590 17/11/46.
63590 1/7/49.

CONDEMNED: 11/7/65.
Sold for scrap to A.Draper,
Hull, 8/65. Cut up 4/10/65.

6244

Gorton, rebuilt from O4/1.

To traffic 15/4/1944.

REPAIRS:
Gor. 13—21/3/45.**G**.
Gor. 8/7—24/8/46.**G**.
Gor. 7/6—7/7/48.**G**.
Gor. 4/9—12/10/50.**G**.
Gor. 18/10—2/11/50.**N/C**.
Gor. 12/1—29/2/52.**C/L**.
Gor. 10—29/11/52.**G**.
Gor. 30/8—2/10/54.**G**.
Gor. 31/8—8/10/55.**C/L**.
Gor. 17—22/11/56.**G**.
Gor. 23/1—22/2/58.**C/L**.
Gor. 25/6—7/8/59.**G**.
Gor. 28/3—10/5/62.**L/I**.

BOILERS:
9430.
5033 *(ex3789)* 7/7/48.
28265 *(ex63768)* 12/10/50.
28386 *(ex63786)* 29/11/52.
28829 *(ex63868)* 2/10/54.
28811 *(exO4/8 63575)* 22/11/56.

Two came from O4 Part 2: Nos.6328 (63725 later) and 6288 (63879 later). Cambridge shed, 1st May 1960.

No less than thirty-eight were from Part 3 of O4 class, those that had been bought from the ROD.

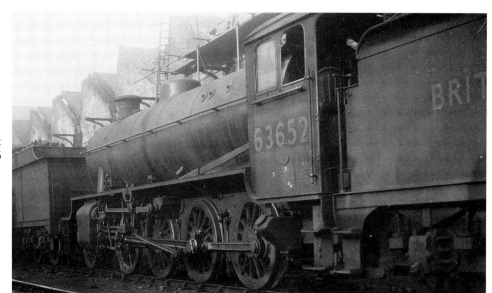

No.6371 had been Part 4 of O4 class. It became No.3652 from 22nd November 1946 and 63652 from 3rd April 1948.

(right) Nos.ᴇ3579 and 63589 were rebuilt from Part 5 of O4 class. Annesley shed, 30th September 1956.

(below) There was also just one, No.63596 (ex 6249), which had been Part 7 from 26th September 1942. The wide difference of appearance in these parts of O4 class, dissolved into the uniform guise of O1 class. Note the high front plate, put on whilst this tender was in the Scottish Area with O4 Part 2 No.6372. No.63596 had this tender from ex works 15th November 1952 to its 29th August 1963 withdrawal. March shed, 26th April 1959.

6244 continued.
28268 *(exO4/8 63683)* 7/8/59.

SHEDS:
Gorton 15/4/44.
New England 15/5/44.
Gorton 25/6/45.
Annesley 26/11/50.

RENUMBERED:
3591 22/12/46.
63591 7/7/48.

CONDEMNED: 17/11/62.
Into Crw. for cut up 9/63.

6245

Gorton, rebuilt from O4/1.

To traffic 5/10/1946.

REPAIRS:
Gor. 26/6—31/7/48.**G.**
Gor. 20/1—3/2/51.**G.**
Gor. 12/4—3/5/52.**G.**
Gor. 6—11/5/52.**N/C.**
Gor. 15/3—17/4/54.**G.**
Gor. 20—27/4/54.**N/C.**
Gor. 27/2—20/4/55.**C/L.**
Gor. 30/6—10/9/55.**C/H.**
Gor. 21/9—3/11/56.**G.**
Gor. 12/12/59—15/1/60.**G.**
Gor. 4—11/3/60.**N/C.**

BOILERS:
5085.
5053 *(ex3773)* 31/7/48.
28806 *(new)* 3/2/51.
28380 *(exO4/8 63802)* 3/5/52.
28824 *(ex63663)* 17/4/54.
28448 *(exB1 61069)* 10/9/55.
28853 *(ex63773)* 3/11/56.
28363 *(ex63863)* 15/1/60.

SHEDS:
Colwick 5/10/46.
Gorton 20/10/46.
Annesley 26/11/50.
Colwick 3/11/57.
Staveley 9/6/63.

RENUMBERED:
3592 18/11/46.
63592 31/7/48.

CONDEMNED: 23/7/63.
Into Don. for cut up 12/8/63.

3594
(ex 5333/3506)

Gorton, rebuilt from O4/1.

To traffic 22/11/1947.

REPAIRS:
Gor. 3/3—9/4/49.**C/L.**
Gor. 27/3—6/5/50.**G.**
Gor. 11/6—11/8/51.**G.**
Gor. 16—21/8/51.**N/C.**
Gor. 6—27/12/52.**G.**
Gor. 30/10—4/12/54.**G.**
Gor. 19/3/55.**N/C.**
Gor. 8/12/56—5/1/57.**G.**
Gor. 10/5—14/6/58.**C/L.**
Gor. 9/1—13/2/60.**G.**

BOILERS:
5111.
5041 *(exO4/8 63575)* 6/5/50.
5041 reno.28332 11/8/51.
28388 *(ex63808)* 27/12/52.
28901 *(new)* 4/12/54.
28299 *(ex63865)* 5/1/57.
28927 *(exO4/8 63675)* 13/2/60.

SHEDS:
Doncaster 22/11/47.
Frodingham 18/1/48.
Mexborough 22/2/48.
Annesley 16/1/49.
Colwick 3/11/57.
Staveley 24/11/63.

RENUMBERED:
63594 9/4/49.

CONDEMNED: 21/4/64.
Sold for scrap to Smiths,
Ecclesfield 5/64.

63596
(ex 6249/3596)

Gorton, rebuilt from O4/7.

To traffic 30/7/1949.

REPAIRS:
Gor. 20/10—10/11/51.**G.**
Gor. 25/10—15/11/52.**C/H.**
Gor. 31/10—21/11/53.**G.**
Gor. 4/12/54—15/1/55.**C/L.**
Gor. 28/1—25/2/56.**G.**
Gor. 14/6—2/8/58.**G.**
Gor. 8/11/58.**C/L.**
Gor. 7/1—15/2/61.**G.**

BOILERS:
5116.
28358 *(ex63792)* 10/11/51.
28332 *(ex63594)* 21/11/53.
28890 *(new)* 25/2/56.
28802 *(exO4/8 63893)* 2/8/58.
28855 *(ex63589)* 15/2/61.

SHEDS:
Annesley 30/7/49.
March 17/2/57.
Staveley 10/1/60.

RENUMBERED:
63596 30/7/49.

CONDEMNED: 29/8/63.
Into Don. for cut up 3/12/63.

5385

Gorton, rebuilt from O4/1.

To traffic 29/7/1944.

REPAIRS:
Gor. 6/8—21/9/46.**G.**
Gor. 20/3—16/4/49.**G.**
S/C smokebox fitted.
Gor. 5/4—4/6/50.**C/H.**
Gor. 19/7—25/8/51.**G.**
Gor. 28/8—25/9/51.**C/L.**
Gor. 9—13/10/51.**N/C.**
Gor. 3—20/6/53.**G.**
Gor. 31/8—25/9/54.**C/L.**
Gor. 11/5—25/6/55.**G.**
Gor. 2/6—28/7/56.**C/H.**
Gor. 13/2—2/3/57.**C/L.**
Gor. 17/9—19/10/57.**G.**
Gor. 20/10—18/11/59.**H/I.**
Gor. 5/9—19/10/62.**G.**

BOILERS:
5005.
5004 *(ex3784)* 21/9/46.
5096 *(exO4/8 3633)* 16/4/49.
28340 *(ex63676)* 25/8/51.
28314 *(ex63755)* 20/6/53.
28284 *(ex63689)* 25/6/55.
28883 *(ex63571)* 19/10/57.
28805 *(ex63803)* 19/10/62.

SHEDS:
Doncaster 29/7/44.
Thornton Jct. 20/8/44.
Annesley 23/1/49.

RENUMBERED:
3610 27/10/46.
63610 14/4/49.

CONDEMNED: 21/11/62.
Into Gor. for cut up 1/63.

5394

Gorton, rebuilt from O4/1.

To traffic 17/3/1945.

REPAIRS:
Gor. 3—31/5/47.**G.**
Gor. 6—20/8/49.**G.**
S/C smokebox fitted.
Gor. 24/1—23/2/52.**G.**
Gor. 30/1—7/3/53.**C/L.**
Gor. 10—14/3/53.**N/C.**
Gor. 20/1—20/2/54.**G.**
Gor. 23/2—16/3/54.**N/C.**
Gor. 6/2—15/3/55.**C/L.**
Gor. 1/5—23/6/56.**G.**
Gor. 7/10—1/11/58.**G.**
Gor. 4/5—10/6/61.**H/I.**

BOILERS:
5030.
5026 *(ex3868)* 31/5/47.
5027 *(exO4/8 3819)* 20/8/49.
28371 *(ex63780)* 23/2/52.
28358 *(ex63596)* 20/2/54.
28359 *(ex63869)* 23/6/56.
28316 *(ex63725)* 1/11/58.

SHEDS:
Annesley 17/3/45.
Gorton 1/4/45.
Annesley 26/11/50.
March 3/3/57.
Staveley 17/1/60.

RENUMBERED:
3619 16/6/46.
63619 20/8/49.

CONDEMNED: 21/10/63.
Sold for scrap to T.W.Ward,
Beighton, 6/64.

6555

Gorton, rebuilt from O4/3.

To traffic 30/6/1945.

REPAIRS:
Gor. 19/4—31/5/47.**G.**
Gor. 14/2/48.**L.**
Gor. 12/6/48.**L.**
Gor. 2/4/49.**C/L.**
Gor. 30/7—27/8/49.**G.**

WORKS CODES:- Bpk - Beyer, Peacock. Crw - Crewe. Cw - Cowlairs. Dar- Darlington. Dby - Derby. Don - Doncaster. Ghd - Gateshead. Gor - Gorton. Inv - Inverurie. Str - Stratford.
REPAIR CODES:- **C/H** - Casual Heavy. **C/L** - Casual Light. **G** - General. **H**- Heavy. **H/I** - Heavy Intermediate. **L** - Light. **L/I** - Light Intermediate. **N/C** - Non-Classified.

198

(above) **The class was introduced whilst wartime air raid precautions still applied, and those rebuilt by May 1945 were equipped with a tarpaulin sheet at the rear edge of the cab roof to screen glare from an open firebox door after dark. No.6624 became O1 from 2nd September 1944. Note steel plate fitted instead of glass in the front windows.**

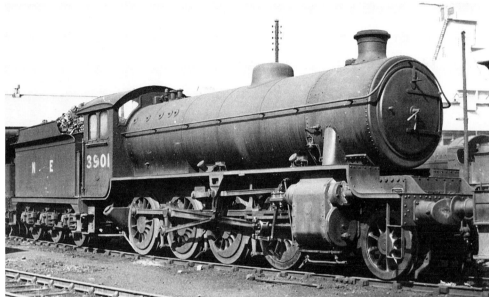

(right) **It was standard practice on the LNER to fit the return crank of the Walschaerts gear with a ball race. Darnall shed.**

During 1944/45 there was difficulty in getting ball bearings and many of the early rebuilds had to make do with a plain bearing for the return crank. No.3786 was No.6515 when rebuilt 18th November 1944, and fifteen got plain bearings: Nos.5385, 5408, 6195, 6243, 6283, 6288, 6350, 6507, 6515, 6519, 6578, 6601, 6624, 6626 and 6630. Mexborough, 19th September 1948.

(left) **There was no uniformity of front coupling. Although essentially goods engines, many had the adjustable screw type. As expected, the others continued to carry the loose three-link type. Gorton works.**

(below) **Although no details were recorded on their history cards in 1947, Nos.3592 and 3777 were fitted with a speed indicator, driven from the right hand trailing coupling pin. Almost certainly they were connected with the 1947 speeding up of the Annesley to Woodford goods and mineral trains. Doncaster shed.**

Lubrication for cylinders and steam chest was from a Wakefield mechanical lubricator on the left hand running plate. For the coupled wheel axleboxes and horn cheeks a central siphon feed lubricator served the three leading wheels, the rear one having a similar oil box located in the cab. Annesley shed, 7th June 1953.

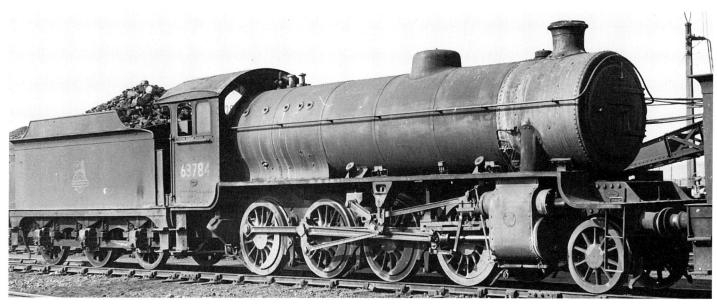

For the axleboxes and horn cheeks there was similar lubrication on the right hand side. Gravity fed sanders served the first and third coupled wheels and the fillers had short shields around them. These were not very effective and were later extended (*see* page 232, top).

(*right*) No.3777 was previously No.6214 which was from O4/1, the Part which was vacuum brake fitted. O1 class was steam brake only, on engine and tender, and so the train pipe connection was taken off on rebuilding. Lincoln shed, 14th July 1947.

(*below*) Removal of water scoop from the tender had begun in the 1930's but the war had slowed progress. When No.3760 was rebuilt 31st August 1946 it was fitted with tender No.6221 which still had a scoop as shown by the operating wheel at the front end on the right hand side.

At rebuilding the majority of O1 class had tenders without a water scoop and removal was resumed post war. Gorton shed.

When No.6624 was rebuilt 2nd September 1944 from O4/3 it was also fitted with a Part 3 tender, which only needed a steam brake to be fitted.

6555 continued.
S/C smokebox fitted.
Gor. 17/2—10/3/51.**C/H.**
Gor. 5—19/4/52.**G.**
Gor. 4—18/4/53.**C/L.**
Gor. 27/3—17/4/54.**G.**
Gor. 26/3—23/4/55.**C/L.**
Gor. 13/8—1/10/55.**C/L.**
After collision.
Gor. 4/8—8/9/56.**G.**
Gor. 18/1/58.**C/L.**
Gor. 20/9—18/10/58.**G.**
Gor. 21/2—7/3/59.**C/L.**
Don. 16/1—10/3/62.**G.**

BOILERS:
5039.
5014 *(ex3590)* 31/5/47.
5105 *(ex3663)* 27/8/49.
5105 reno.28299 10/3/51.
28828 *(new)* 19/4/52.
28341 *(exO4/8 63819)* 17/4/54.
28339 *(ex63579)* 8/9/56.
28975 *(new)* 18/10/58.

SHEDS:
Mexborough 30/6/45.
Gorton 8/7/45.
Woodford 18/8/46.
Gorton 20/10/46.
Annesley 26/11/50.
March 3/3/57.
Staveley 24/1/60.
Langwith Jct. 13/6/65.

RENUMBERED:
3630 9/11/46.
63630 12/6/48.

CONDEMNED: 11/7/65.
Sold for scrap to A.Draper, Hull, 8/65. Cut up 25/10/65.

6374

Gorton, rebuilt from O4/3.

To traffic 15/9/1945.

REPAIRS:
Gor. ?/?—?/2/46.**L.**
Drop grate fitted.
Gor. 27/4—4/5/46.**L.**
After collision.
Gor. 15—22/6/46.**L.**
After collision.
Gor. 26/7—16/8/47.**G.**
Gor. 9—14/2/48.**L.**
Gor. 7/5/49.**C/L.**
Gor. 25/2—11/3/50.**G.**
Gor. 29/3—19/4/52.**G.**
Gor. 18/4—9/5/53.**C/L.**
Gor. 13/2—6/3/54.**G.**
Gor. 12/2—12/3/55.**C/L.**

Gor. 7/4—5/5/56.**G.**
Gor. 12/7—30/8/58.**G.**
Don. 4/5—10/7/62.**G.**
Don. 18/7—3/8/62.**C/L.**

BOILERS:
5043.
5035 *(ex3650)* 16/8/47.
5113 *(ex3578)* 11/3/50.
28377 *(ex63795)* 19/4/52.
28297 *(ex63838)* 6/3/54.
28379 *(ex63789)* 5/5/56.
28851 *(ex63780)* 30/8/58.
28265 *(ex63746)* 10/7/62.

SHEDS:
Langwith Jct. 15/9/45.
Gorton 23/9/45.
Woodford 18/8/46.
Gorton 20/10/46.
Annesley 2/7/50.
March 24/2/57.
Staveley 31/1/60.
Langwith Jct. 13/6/65.

RENUMBERED:
3646 1/12/46.
ᴇ**3646** 14/2/48.
63646 7/5/49.

CONDEMNED: 11/7/65.
Sold for scrap to A.Draper, Hull, 8/65. Cut up 4/10/65.

6545

Gorton, rebuilt from O4/3.

To traffic 26/5/1945.

REPAIRS:
Gor. 7—28/6/47.**G.**
Gor. 13/8—3/9/49.**G.**
S/C smokebox fitted.
Gor. 2—23/2/52.**G.**
Gor. 26/9—17/10/53.**G.**
Gor. 19/6—3/7/54.**C/L.**
Gor. 1—29/10/55.**G.**
Gor. 28/12/57—1/2/58.**G.**
Gor. 13/12/58.**N/C.**
Gor. 4/2—11/3/61.**G.**
Don. 20/2—19/3/63.**C/H.**

BOILERS:
5035.
5031 *(ex3725)* 28/6/47.
5011 *(exO4/8 3653)* 3/9/49.
28372 *(ex63711)* 23/2/52.
28325 *(ex63578)* 17/10/53.
28809 *(ex63777)* 29/10/55.
28824 *(ex63687)* 1/2/58.
28299 *(ex63594)* 11/3/61.
28983 *(ex63863)* 19/3/63.

SHEDS:
Doncaster 26/5/45.
Gorton 3/6/45.
Colwick 18/8/46.
Gorton 20/10/46.
Annesley 26/11/50.
March 17/2/57.
Staveley 7/2/60.
Langwith Jct. 13/6/65.

RENUMBERED:
3650 2/11/46.
63650 3/9/49.

CONDEMNED: 27/6/65.
Sold for scrap to R.A.King, Norwich, 8/65.

6371

Gorton, rebuilt from O4/4.

To traffic 15/12/1945.

REPAIRS:
Gor. ?/?—?/2/46.**L.**
Drop grate fitted.
Gor. 13/3—3/4/48.**G.**
Gor. 26/8—16/9/50.**G.**
Gor. 31/5—14/6/52.**G.**
Gor. 20/6—4/7/53.**C/L.**
Gor. 15/5—5/6/54.**G.**
Gor. 28/5—2/7/55.**C/L.**
Gor. 16/6—4/8/56.**G.**
Gor. 13/9—18/10/58.**G.**
Don. 5/2—21/4/62.**G.**

BOILERS:
5048.
5046 *(ex3752)* 3/4/48.
28257 *(ex63872)* 16/9/50.
28299 *(ex63630)* 14/6/52.
28380 *(ex63592)* 5/6/54.
28371 *(ex63687)* 4/8/56.
28377 *(exO4/8 63828)* 18/10/58.
28895 *(exO4/8 63873)* 21/4/62.

SHEDS:
Langwith Jct. 15/12/45.
Gorton 6/1/46.
Colwick 18/8/46.
Gorton 20/10/46.
Annesley 26/11/50.
March 10/2/57.
Staveley 14/2/60.
Colwick 7/10/62.
Staveley 9/6/63.

RENUMBERED:
3652 22/11/46.
63652 3/4/48.

CONDEMNED: 11/11/63.
Sold for scrap to T.W.Ward, Beighton, 4/64.

6359

Gorton, rebuilt from O4/3.

To traffic 16/6/1945.

REPAIRS:
Gor. 3—31/5/47.**G.**
Gor. 25/6—6/8/49.**G.**
S/C smokebox fitted.
Gor. 19/1—9/2/52.**G.**
Gor. 3—17/5/52.**C/L.**
Gor. 14—28/11/53.**G.**
Gor. 15/1—5/2/55.**C/L.**
Gor. 19/11—24/12/55.**G.**
Gor. 14/9—5/10/57.**G.**
Don. 24/4—9/6/62.**G.**

BOILERS:
5038.
5105 *(new)* 31/5/47.
5036 *(ex3590)* 6/8/49.
28824 *(new)* 9/2/52.
28316 *(ex63676)* 28/11/53.
28283 *(ex63795)* 24/12/55.
28812 *(ex63886)* 5/10/57.
28809 *(exO4/8 63781)* 9/6/62.

SHEDS:
Retford 16/6/45.
Gorton 8/7/45.
Colwick 18/8/46.
Gorton 20/10/46.
Annesley 26/11/50.
March 24/2/57.
Staveley 22/11/59.
Colwick 7/10/62.
Staveley 9/6/63.

RENUMBERED:
3663 2/11/46.
63663 6/8/49.

CONDEMNED: 1/11/64.
Sold for scrap to Thompson's, Stockton-on-Tees, 12/65.

6356

Gorton, rebuilt from O4/3.

To traffic 16/3/1946.

REPAIRS:
Gor. ?/?—?/4/46.**L.**
Drop grate fitted.
Gor. 8—29/11/47.**G.**
Gor. 4/9/48.**L.**
Gor. 22/1/49.**L.**

6356 continued.
Gor. 10/12/49.**L.**
Gor. 13—27/5/50.**G.**
Gor. 31/5—21/6/52.**G.**
Gor. 8—29/5/54.**G.**
Gor. 14/5—4/6/55.**G.**
Gor. 2—30/6/56.**C/H.**
Gor. 9/8—20/9/58.**G.**
Gor. 14/1—18/2/61.**G.**

BOILERS:
  5052.
  5040 *(ex3740)* 29/11/47.
  5032 *(ex63752)* 27/5/50.
  28830 *(new)* 21/6/52.
  28828 *(ex63630)* 29/5/54.
  28289 *(ex63803)* 30/6/56.
  28973 *(new)* 20/9/58.
  28853 *(ex63592)* 18/2/61.

SHEDS:
Langwith Jct. 16/3/46.
Frodingham 7/4/46.
Gorton 12/5/46.
Colwick 18/8/46.
Gorton 20/10/46.
Annesley 26/11/50.
March 10/2/57.
Staveley 21/2/60.

RENUMBERED:
  3670 8/9/46.
  63670 4/9/48.

CONDEMNED: 4/6/64.
Sold for scrap to T.W.Ward,
Killamarsh, 8/64.

_____

6350

Gorton, rebuilt from O4/3.

To traffic 27/1/1945.

REPAIRS:
Gor. 1—24/8/46.**G.**
Gor. 18/3—14/4/49.**G.**
Gor. 12/4—12/5/51.**G.**
Gor. 3—28/2/53.**G.**
Gor. 15/2—13/3/54.**C/L.**
Gor. 25/4—28/5/55.**G.**
Gor. 26/4—25/5/57.**G.**
Gor. 3/11—8/12/59.**H/I.**
Gor. 8/8—21/9/62.**G.**

BOILERS:
  5020.
  5006 *(ex6601)* 24/8/46.
  5083 *(ex3874)* 14/4/49.
  28316 *(ex63773)* 12/5/51.
  28393 *(ex63901)* 28/2/53.
  28389 *(exO4/8 63853)* 28/5/55.
  28840 *(ex63740)* 25/5/57.
  28355 *(ex63712)* 21/9/62.

SHEDS:
West Hartlepool 27/1/45.
Hull Springhead 2/3/45.
Hull Dairycoates 4/6/45.
Tyne Dock 26/8/46.
Darlington 6/2/49.
Hull Dairycoates 11/9/49.
Hull Springhead 5/2/50.
Hull Dairycoates 21/5/50.
Annesley 2/9/51.

RENUMBERED:
  3676 24/11/46.
  63676 14/4/49.

CONDEMNED: 21/11/62.
Into Gor. for cut up 12/62.

_____

5408

Gorton, rebuilt from O4/1.

To traffic 23/12/1944.

REPAIRS:
Gor. 7—28/12/46.**G.**
Gor. 1—4/9/48.**C/L.**
Gor. 26/3—14/5/49.**G.**
Gor. 22/4/50.**C/L.**
Gor. 22/11—29/12/51.**G.**
Gor. 14/2—13/3/54.**G.**
Gor. 16—26/3/54.**N/C.**
Gor. 2/10—24/11/55.**C/L.**
Gor. 15/3—21/4/56.**G.**
Gor. 27/1—1/3/58.**G.**
Gor. 30/6—13/8/60.**H/I.**

BOILERS:
  5018.
  5022 *(ex3792)* 28/12/46.
  5006 *(ex3676)* 14/5/49.
  28367 *(ex63596)* 29/12/51.
  28343 *(ex63856)* 13/3/54.
  28893 *(new)* 21/4/56.
  28839 *(ex63795)* 1/3/58.

SHEDS:
Annesley 23/12/44.
Gorton 7/1/45.
Annesley 26/11/50.
March 24/2/57.
Staveley 28/2/60.

RENUMBERED:
  3529 1/9/46.
  3678 26/2/47.
  63678 4/9/48.

CONDEMNED: 18/7/63.
Into Don. for cut up 12/8/63.

_____

6324

Gorton, rebuilt from O4/3.

To traffic 29/12/1945.

REPAIRS:
Gor. ?/?—?/2/46.**L.**
Drop grate fitted.
Gor. 6—27/12/47.**G.**
Gor. 25/6/49.**C/L.**
Gor. 18/3—1/4/50.**G.**
Gor. 29/3—12/4/52.**G.**
Gor. 7/8—4/9/54.**G.**
Gor. 6/8—10/9/55.**C/L.**
Gor. 2/6—7/7/56.**G.**
Gor. 23/8—20/9/58.**G.**
Gor. 9/4/60.**N/C.**
Gor. 22/4—3/6/61.**H/I.**
AWS fitted.
Gor. 13—27/1/62.**C/L.**
Don. 30/7—2/8/62.**C/L.**

BOILERS:
  5032.
  5052 *(ex3670)* 27/12/47.
  5100 *(ex63579)* 1/4/50.
  28805 *(ex63890)* 12/4/52.
  28371 *(ex63619)* 4/9/54.
  28336 *(ex63887)* 7/7/56.
  28314 *(ex63590)* 20/9/58.

SHEDS:
Retford 29/12/45.
Gorton 6/1/46.
Colwick 18/8/46.
Gorton 20/10/46.
Annesley 19/2/48.
Gorton 7/3/48.
Annesley 23/4/50.
March 10/2/57.

RENUMBERED:
  3687 2/11/46.
  63687 25/6/49.

CONDEMNED: 16/10/63.
Into Don. for cut up 30/1/64.

_____

6341

Gorton, rebuilt from O4/3.

To traffic 11/8/1945.

REPAIRS:
Gor. 6/7—7/8/47.**G.**
Gor. 5/9—8/10/49.**G.**
Gor. 22/4—26/5/51.**G.**
Gor. 30/5—3/6/51.**N/C.**
Gor. 5—28/2/53.**G.**
Gor. 20/4—9/5/53.**C/L.**
Gor. 24/3—23/4/54.**C/L.**
Gor. 2/3—7/4/55.**G.**

Gor. 16/6—2/7/55.**C/L.**
Gor. 5/3—20/4/56.**C/L.**
Gor. 13/3—13/4/57.**G.**
Gor. 9/7—21/8/59.**H/I.**
Gor. 8—11/9/59.**N/C.**
Gor. 15/6—8/7/60.**C/L.**
Gor. 2/3—12/4/62.**G.**

BOILERS:
  5041.
  5034 *(ex3780)* 7/8/47.
  5084 *(ex3755)* 8/10/49.
  28812 *(new)* 26/5/51.
  28284 *(ex63784)* 28/2/53.
  28257 *(ex63578)* 7/4/55.
  28390 *(ex63867)* 13/4/57.
  28383 *(ex63865)* 12/4/62.

SHEDS:
Gorton 11/8/45.
Colwick 18/8/46.
Gorton 20/10/46.
Annesley 16/7/50.

RENUMBERED:
  3689 11/11/46.
  63689 8/10/49.

CONDEMNED: 17/11/62.
Into Crw. for cut up 9/63.

_____

6195

Gorton, rebuilt from O4/1.

To traffic 10/10/1944.

REPAIRS:
Gor. 11—14/10/44.**N/C.**
Gor. 20/10—30/11/46.**G.**
Gor. 7/6—1/7/49.**G.**
Gor. 11/10—24/11/51.**G.**
Gor. 27/11—3/12/51.**N/C.**
Gor. 30/9—31/10/53.**G.**
Gor. 22/10—27/11/54.**C/L.**
Gor. 30/3—7/4/55.**N/C.**
Gor. 12/11—17/12/55.**G.**
Gor. 9/11—7/12/57.**G.**
Gor. 30/5—2/8/58.**L.**
Boiler repairs.
Gor. 12/1—18/2/61.**H/I.**
Gor. 27/4—10/8/62.**C/H.**

BOILERS:
  5009.
  5015 *(exO4/8 3802)* 1/7/49.
  28362 *(exO4/8 63633)* 24/11/51.
  28339 *(ex63740)* 31/10/53.
  28325 *(ex63650)* 17/12/55.
  28284 *(ex63610)* 7/12/57.
  28824 *(ex63650)* 10/8/62.

SHEDS:
Mexborough 10/10/44.

In 1952 five were fitted for working the block trains of bogie wagons carrying iron ore from Tyne Dock to Consett. These trains were vacuum braked so a vacuum ejector had to be fitted and the steam brake valve changed to a graduable type. No.63712 was so fitted ex works 26th April 1952. Tyne Dock, 17th May 1954.

The bogie wagons had air operated doors which had to be opened whilst on the move over the gantry at Consett. A Westinghouse pump to supply compressed air to open the doors was mounted on the right hand side of the firebox. No.63755 was fitted ex Gorton 5th July 1952. Tyne Dock shed, September 1953.

The wagon doors were held in the closed position by a separate air system which another Westinghouse pump supplied. This too was mounted on the right hand side of the firebox. No.63760 was fitted 26th July 1952. Note that the wider sand filler protection plates had been put on.

(above) The 10in. Westinghouse pumps fitted on these five engines came from former WD 'Austerity' 2-8-0 engines. No.63856 was equipped for iron ore train working ex Gorton on 17th May 1952. Tyne Dock shed, May 1960.

(left) The fifth engine to have this special equipment was 63874, ex works 18th October 1952. All five kept it until withdrawn together on 26th November 1962. Tyne Dock shed.

Until they were shopped in the mid 1950's, no O1 had been provided with hinged glass screens on the cab sides. Some, but not all, were then fitted with them. Pages 232 top and 241 top, show 63868 and 63663 still without them late in 1962.

(below) Standard brake was steam only on the engine and tender with no provision for train braking. Gorton.

Late in their life, six O1's were fitted with BR AWS. This needed a BR type vacuum ejector, fitted on the left-hand side of the smokebox and through train piping. The six were 63687 (3rd June 1961), 63712 (8th September 1962), 63780 (14th October 1961), 63838 (31st January 1962), 63868 (14th October 1961), and 63890 (3rd February 1962). Note no front standpipe was provided.

For the AWS a vacuum reservoir was put on the right hand running plate just in front of the cab, and a sloping protection plate avoided damage to the electrical receiver from a swinging front coupling. On the left-hand side, under the cab, a battery box was added. March shed, 7th October 1962.

(above) The AWS battery box was fitted between the trailing sandbox and the cab footstep. March shed, 2nd June 1963.

(left) Along with the AWS equipment, these six had adjustable screw coupling fitted. Gainsborough Lea Road.

3542 continued.
Gorton 15/10/44.
Annesley 26/11/50.

RENUMBERED:
3542 19/10/46.
3711 27/3/47.
63711 1/7/49.

CONDEMNED: 17/11/62.
Into Crw. for cut up 9/63.

6334

Gorton, rebuilt from O4/3.

To traffic 13/5/1944.

REPAIRS:
Gor. 28/9—26/10/46.**G.**
Gor. 29/1—12/2/49.**G.**
S/C smokebox fitted.
Gor. ?/?—6/10/49.**C/L.**
Gor. 8/9—6/10/51.**G.**
Gor. 15/3—26/4/52.**C/L.**
*Westinghouse pumps & vacuum
ejector fittted for working iron
ore traffic.*
Gor. 15—29/11/52.**C/L.**
New L.H. cylinder.
Gor. 20/3—17/4/54.**G.**
Gor. 24/11—22/12/56.**G.**
Gor. 9/1—20/2/60.**H/I.**
Gor. 7/7—8/9/62.**G.**
AWS fitted.
Gor. 13—23/11/62.**N/C.**

BOILERS:
9432.
   5005 (*ex5385*) 26/10/46.
   5008 (*ex3806*) 12/2/49.
28350 (*ex63886*) 6/10/51.
28832 (*ex63590*) 17/4/54.
28355 (*exO4/8 63613*) 22/12/56.
28842 (*exO4/8 63653*) 8/9/62.

SHEDS:
Immingham 13/5/44.
Gorton 21/5/44.
Tyne Dock 11/6/44.
Hull Springhead 18/6/45.
Tyne Dock 21/3/46.
Darlington 6/2/49.
Hull Dairycoates 11/9/49.
Hull Springhead 5/2/50.
Hull Dairycoates 21/5/50.
Tyne Dock 2/9/51.

RENUMBERED:
3712 1/9/46.
63712 12/2/49.

CONDEMNED: 26/11/62.
Into Gor. for cut up 12/62.

6328

Gorton, rebuilt from O4/2.

To traffic 31/3/1945.

REPAIRS:
Gor. 3—24/5/47.**G.**
Gor. 6—20/8/49.**G.**
S/C smokebox fitted.
Gor. 3/11—1/12/51.**G.**
Gor. 22/11—27/12/52.**C/H.**
Gor. 28/11—19/12/53.**G.**
Gor. 18/12/54—22/1/55.**C/L.**
Gor. 28/1—25/2/56.**G.**
Gor. 30/8—27/9/58.**G.**
Gor. 24/1—7/2/59.**C/L.**
Gor. 19/12/59—16/1/60.**C/L.**
Don. 19/6—30/8/62.**G.**

BOILERS:
5031.
   5081 (*new*) 24/5/47.
   5009 (*ex3711*) 20/8/49.
28363 (*ex63712*) 1/12/51.
28351 (*ex63795*) 19/12/53.
28316 (*ex63663*) 25/2/56.
28289 (*ex63670*) 27/9/58.
28300 (*exO2/4 63955*) 30/8/62.

SHEDS:
Langwith Jct. 31/3/45.
Gorton 15/4/45.
Colwick 18/8/46.
Gorton 20/10/46.
Annesley 26/11/50.
Wellingborough 15/7/56.
Annesley 16/12/56.
March 24/2/57.
Staveley 24/11/63.
Barrow Hill 13/6/65.

RENUMBERED:
3725 9/6/46.
63725 20/8/49.

CONDEMNED: 11/7/65.
*Sold for scrap to A.Draper,
Hull. Cut up 4/10/65.*

6566

Gorton, rebuilt from O4/3.

To traffic 4/8/1945.

REPAIRS:
Gor. 1/10—1/11/47.**G.**
Gor. 25/3—3/4/48.**L.**
Gor. 10—26/6/48.**L.**
Gor. 2—12/2/49.**C/L.**
Gor. 22/3—23/4/49.**C/H.**
Gor. 8/11—10/12/49.**C/H.**
Gor. 25/1—3/3/51.**G.**

Gor. 23/1—14/2/53.**G.**
Gor. 20/8—12/9/53.**C/H.**
Gor. 17/3—21/4/55.**G.**
Gor. 6/2—16/3/57.**G.**
Gor. 15/9—23/10/59.**G.**
Gor. 26/6—16/8/62.**H/I.**

BOILERS:
5040.
   5037 (*ex3803*) 1/11/47.
28295 (*ex63784*) 3/3/51.
28839 (*new*) 14/2/53.
28274 (*ex63590*) 12/9/53.
28840 (*ex63589*) 21/4/55.
28386 (*ex63784*) 16/3/57.
28984 (*new*) 23/10/59.

SHEDS:
Hull Dairycoates 4/8/45.
Tyne Dock 31/3/46.
Darlington 6/2/49.
Hull Dairycoates 11/9/49.
Hull Springhead 5/2/50.
Hull Dairycoates 21/5/50.
Annesley 2/9/51.

RENUMBERED:
3740 17/5/46.
63740 3/4/48.

CONDEMNED: 17/11/62.
Into Crw. for cut up 9/63.

63746
(ex 6571/3746)

Gorton, rebuilt from O4/3.

To traffic 27/11/1948.

REPAIRS:
Gor. 8—15/10/49.**C/H.**
Gor. 14/10—4/11/50.**G.**
Gor. 5—19/5/51.**C/H.**
Gor. 8—15/3/52.**C/L.**
Gor. 18/10—1/11/52.**G.**
Gor. 9—16/5/53.**C/L.**
Gor. 31/7—4/9/54.**G.**
Gor. 25/6—30/7/55.**C/L.**
Gor. 1/9—6/10/56.**G.**
Gor. 31/8—7/9/57.**C/L.**
Gor. 27/9—25/10/58.**G.**
Don. 9/4—22/5/62.**G.**
Don. 15/6—2/7/62.**N/C.**

BOILERS:
5117.
28273 (*ex63591*) 4/11/50.
28385 (*exO4/8 63836*) 1/11/52.
28383 (*ex63863*) 4/9/54.
28828 (*ex63670*) 6/10/56.
28265 (*exO4/8 63728*) 25/10/58.
28831 (*ex63773*) 22/5/62.

SHEDS:
Staveley 27/11/48.
Annesley 5/12/48.
March 3/3/57.
Staveley 24/11/63.

RENUMBERED:
63746 27/11/48.

CONDEMNED: 27/2/64.
*Sold for scrap to T.W.Ward,
Beighton, 6/64.*

6575

Gorton, rebuilt from O4/3.

To traffic 17/11/1945.

REPAIRS:
Gor. ?/?—?/2/46.**L.**
Drop grate fitted.
Gor. 1—30/1/48.**G.**
Gor. 11—13/11/48.**L.**
Gor. 14—23/3/49.**N/C.**
Gor. 3/4—6/5/50.**G.**
Gor. 6—30/6/51.**C/H.**
Gor. 11/9—4/10/52.**G.**
Gor. 11/9—17/10/53.**C/L.**
Gor. 13/12/54—3/2/55.**G.**
Gor. 30/1—28/2/57.**G.**
Gor. 11/12/58—24/1/59.**C/H.**
Gor. 12/4—18/5/61.**H/I.**
Gor. 7/11—2/12/61.**C/L.**

BOILERS:
5046.
   5032 (*ex3687*) 30/1/48.
   5024 (*ex3901*) 6/5/50.
28329 (*ex63689*) 30/6/51.
28298 (*ex63789*) 4/10/52.
28350 (*ex63712*) 3/2/55.
28329 (*ex63872*) 28/2/57.

SHEDS:
Ardsley 17/11/45.
Gorton 25/11/45.
Woodford 18/8/46.
Gorton 20/10/46.
Annesley 20/2/48.
Gorton 7/3/48.
Annesley 2/7/50.

RENUMBERED:
3752 13/4/46.
E3752 30/1/48.
63752 13/11/48.

CONDEMNED: 17/11/62.
Into Dby. for cut up 6/63.

(*left*) Some not fitted with AWS did have screw coupling (*see* 63650 at foot of page) but the majority had, and retained the 3-link loose coupling. Gainsborough Lea Road.

(*below*) Many retained their GCR type buffers (*see* page 224, bottom) and where replacement by Group Standard type was made, the oval heads were still fitted. 63854 was condemned in November 1962 and here at Annesley in April 1963, in the company of other withdrawn O1's, it is waiting to undertake its final journey to Crewe works for scrapping.

It was unusual for a pair of buffers to differ in style but the GS type on 63650 had one oval and one elliptical head when ex Gorton 11th March 1961. Staveley shed, 17th June 1961.

No.3768 had a change of tender in November 1946 and again in April 1947. It was not uncommon for Gorton to run a trial trip before a tender had been lettered. Guide Bridge.

Throughout their twenty-one years all were painted black without any lining being applied, either by the LNER or BR. The first rebuild was only painted in shop grey for the official photograph (*see* Introduction). Gorton works yard.

When the re-numbering scheme was formulated in July 1943, Class O1 had not come into being. When it did in 1946, the rebuilds took the same numbers as if they had remained in Class O4. Thus, the fifty-eight engines ranged from (6)3571 to 3901.

(left) No.6359 became 3663 on Saturday, 2nd November 1946 at Gorton shed whilst it still had only NE on its tender, although just about unseen due to lack of cleaning. Gorton shed.

(below) No.6350 had LNER restored in shaded transfers when ex works 24th August 1946. It became 3676 on Sunday, 24th November 1946 at Tyne Dock shed in painted figures, without shading.

No.3676 remained as above until it went to Gorton for repair on 18th March 1949. Ex works on the 14th April 1949, it had acquired a smokebox numberplate on which the 6 was still in the modified style despite being painted in correct Gill sans on the cab sides. Darlington shed, 12th June 1949.

During the two months of 1948 when the BR regional E prefix was being applied, five O1 acquired it. From a general repair on 30th January 1948, No.3752 had it combined with LNER. Nos.3646 (14th February) and 3784 (13th March), got it at light repairs and almost surely keeping LNER on the tender. Nos.E3865 (23rd February) and E3579 (13th March, newly rebuilt) got BRITISH RAILWAYS.

No.E3752 went into works on the 11th November 1948 for a light repair and when out two days later had its 63752 BR number, with correct Gills sans 6, but without having prefix letter E obliterated. Gorton shed.

Whilst Gorton went straight to the ultimate standard 10in. lettering on the tender, at first they still used 12in. figures on the cab. 63652 (3rd) and 63773 (17th), both April 1948, were in that style. Old Oak Common, 1948.

(below, centre) From August 1948 to August 1949 this was standard style with matching 10in. letters and figures.

(bottom) From September 1949 to April 1957 the emblem was in use and all acquired it. Annesley shed, 8th August 1954.

6578

Gorton, rebuilt from O4/3.

To traffic 21/10/1944.

REPAIRS:
Gor. 23/5—6/7/46.**G**.
Gor. 22/7—27/8/49.**G**.
S/C smokebox fitted.
Gor. 20/3—28/4/51.**C/H**.
Gor. 6/6—5/7/52.**G**.
Westinghouse pumps & vacuum ejector fitted for working iron ore traffic.
Ghd. 7—24/5/54.**C/L**.
Gor. 26/11—12/2/55.**G**.
Gor. 25/7—5/10/57.**G**.
Gor. 22/4—31/5/58.**C/L**.
Gor. 24/2—9/4/60.**H/I**.

BOILERS:
5008.
5084 *(new)* 6/7/46.
5014 *(ex63630)* 27/8/49.
28314 *(ex63740)* 28/4/51.
28382 *(ex63725)* 5/7/52.
28365 *(exO4/8 63827)* 12/2/55.
28335 *(ex63856)* 5/10/57.

SHEDS:
West Hartlepool 21/10/44.
Hull Springhead 9/2/45.
Tyne Dock 15/6/46.
Darlington 6/2/49.
Hull Dairycoates 11/9/49.
Hull Springhead 5/2/50.
Hull Dairycoates 21/5/50.
Tyne Dock 2/9/51.

RENUMBERED:
3755 6/7/46.
63755 26/8/49.

CONDEMNED: 26/11/62.
Into Gor. for cut up 3/63.

3760
(ex 6579)

Gorton, rebuilt from O4/3.

To traffic 31/8/1946.

REPAIRS:
Gor. 4/5—4/6/49.**G**.
Gor. 26/7—1/9/51.**G**.
Gor. 9/5—7/6/52.**C/L**.
Vacuum ejector fitted.
Gor. 15—26/7/52.**C/L**.

Westinghouse pumps fitted for working iron ore traffic.
Gor. 1/9—3/10/53.**G**.
Gor. 29/12/55—8/3/56.**G**.
Gor. 19/6—18/8/56.**C/L**.
Gor. 20/8—4/10/58.**G**.
Gor. 29/6—13/8/60.**C/L**.
Gor. 8/8—30/9/61.**L/I**.

BOILERS:
5082.
5022 *(ex63678)* 4/6/49.
28339 *(ex63752)* 1/9/51.
28273 *(ex63746)* 3/10/53.
28310 *(ex63792)* 8/3/56.
28974 *(new)* 4/10/58.

SHEDS:
Tyne Dock 31/8/46.
Darlington 6/2/49.
Hull Dairycoates 11/9/49.
Hull Springhead 5/2/50.
Hull Dairycoates 21/5/50.
Tyne Dock 2/9/51.

RENUMBERED:
3760 30/8/46.
63760 4/6/49.

CONDEMNED: 26/11/62.
Into Gor. for cut up 5/63.

6513

Gorton, rebuilt from O4/3.

To traffic 1/12/1945.

REPAIRS:
Gor. ?/?—?/2/46.**L**.
Drop grate fitted.
Gor. 13/4/46.**L**.
Gor. 21/12/46.**L**.
Gor. 1—29/5/48.**G**.
Gor. 19/8—9/9/50.**G**.
Gor. 2—9/6/51.**C/L**.
Gor. 29/11—13/12/52.**G**.
Gor. 5—26/12/53.**C/L**.
Gor. 28/9—30/10/54.**G**.
Gor. 3/9—1/10/55.**C/L**.
Gor. 22/12/56—19/1/57.**G**.
Gor. 11/4—9/5/59.**G**.
Gor. 18—30/9/59.**N/C**.
Gor. 9—16/1/60.**N/C**.
Don. 27/9—20/11/62.**C/H**.
Dar. 16/11/64—15/1/65.**C/L**.

BOILERS:
5047.
5056 *(ex3872)* 29/5/48.

28253 *(ex3865)* 9/9/50.
28329 *(ex63752)* 13/12/52.
28855 *(new)* 30/10/54.
28448 *(ex63592)* 19/1/57.
28899 *(ex63773)* 9/5/59.
28289 *(ex63725)* 20/11/62.

SHEDS:
Retford 1/12/45.
Gorton 16/12/45.
Colwick 18/8/46.
Gorton 20/10/46.
Annesley 26/11/50.
Colwick 3/11/57.
Staveley 9/6/63.
Langwith Jct. 13/6/65.

RENUMBERED:
3768 30/6/46.
63768 29/5/48.

CONDEMNED: 11/7/65.
Sold for scrap to A.Draper, Hull, 8/65. Cut up 1/11/65.

6213

Gorton, rebuilt from O4/1.

To traffic 6/4/1946.

REPAIRS:
Gor. 20/3—17/4/48.**G**.
Gor. 5/3/49.**L**.
Gor. 26/11/49.**L**.
Gor. 11/2/50.**C/L**.
Gor. 10/3—7/4/51.**G**.
Gor. 27/12/52—17/1/53.**G**.
Gor. 18/9—16/10/54.**G**.
Gor. 13/8—17/9/55.**C/L**.
Gor. 30/6—11/8/56.**G**.
Gor. 15/11—13/12/58.**G**.
Gor. 26/8—7/10/61.**G**.

BOILERS:
5053.
5042 *(ex3863)* 17/4/48.
28303 *(ex63589)* 7/4/51.
28390 *(ex63803)* 17/1/53.
28853 *(new)* 16/10/54.
28899 *(new)* 11/8/56.
28831 *(exO4/8 63628)* 13/12/58.
28944 *(exO4/8 63573)* 7/10/61.

SHEDS:
Staveley 6/4/46.
Frodingham 14/4/46.
Gorton 12/5/46.
Colwick 18/8/46.
Gorton 20/10/46.

Hornsey 2/7/48.
Gorton 5/9/48.
Annesley 26/11/50.
March 24/2/57.
Staveley 29/11/59.

RENUMBERED:
3560 18/11/46.
3773 6/3/47.
63773 17/4/48.

CONDEMNED: 18/10/64.
Sold for scrap to T.W.Ward, Killamarsh, 12/64.

6214

Gorton, rebuilt from O4/1.

To traffic 2/11/1946.

REPAIRS:
Gor. 21/9—15/10/47.**L**.
Gor. 4—30/4/49.**G**.
Gor. 24/6—11/8/51.**G**.
Gor. 14—28/8/51.**N/C**.
Gor. 31/7—5/9/53.**G**.
Gor. 10/9—2/10/54.**C/L**.
Gor. 6/7—20/8/55.**G**.
Gor. 28/11—3/12/55.**C/L**.
Gor. 30/11—15/12/56.**N/C**.
Gor. 15/6—13/7/57.**G**.
Gor. 6/10—17/11/60.**H/I**.

BOILERS:
5086.
5005 *(ex3712)* 30/4/49.
28813 *(new)* 11/8/51.
28809 *(ex63887)* 5/9/53.
28132 *(exB1 61192)* 20/8/55.
28275 *(ex63789)* 13/7/57.

SHEDS:
Doncaster 2/11/46.
Gorton 3/11/46.
Annesley 20/10/50.

RENUMBERED:
3561 29/11/46.
3777 27/3/47.
63777 30/4/49.

CONDEMNED: 26/10/62.
Into Crw. for cut up 9/63.

WORKS CODES:- Bpk - Beyer, Peacock. Crw - Crewe. Cw - Cowlairs. Dar- Darlington. Dby - Derby. Don - Doncaster. Ghd - Gateshead. Gor - Gorton. Inv - Inverurie. Str - Stratford.
REPAIR CODES:- **C/H** - Casual Heavy. **C/L** - Casual Light. **G** - General. **H**- Heavy. **H/I** - Heavy Intermediate. **L** - Light. **L/I** - Light Intermediate. **N/C** - Non-Classified.

216

(*above*) **From April 1957 all fifty-eight had at least one repaint at which the BR crest was put on. Note the SC plate to indicate a self-cleaning smokebox. Staveley, 1st July 1962.**

(*right*) **No.63789 got the crest with lion facing the wrong way when ex works on 22nd June 1957. This was corrected - as shown here on the 30th August 1959, when it was ex works on 10th July 1959. Note the smokebox plate still has LNER modified version of Gill sans figures 6 and 9. Annesley, 30th August 1959.**

Smokebox plates were cast with correct 6 and 9 but 63652, ex works on 16th September 1950, would be one of the last to be fitted. Plates had not started to be put on when it was previously ex works on 3rd April 1948. Cambridge shed.

No.63755 is seen here in August 1950 at Croft Junction, Darlington on a down main line Class A train of empty coal wagons. It was shedded at Dairycoates at this time, but moved to Tyne Dock 2nd September 1951 and was equipped in July 1952 for working the Consett iron ore traffic.

Numbered 63773 from 17th April 1948, it had been 3773 from 6th March 1947, 3560 from 18th November 1946 and 6213 at its 6th April 1946 rebuilding. On 14th April 1946 it left Staveley for Frodingham, went to Gorton 12th May 1946, to Colwick on 18th August 1946 but back to Gorton on 20th October 1946. Chosen to take part in the 1948 Locomotive Exchange trials, it moved to Hornsey shed on the 2nd July 1948 and here on the 31st August 1948 it is leaving the Western Region sidings at Acton with the 11.20 a.m. Class A goods to South Wales. It returned to Gorton on the 5th September 1948.

No.63856 was at Tyne Dock shed from 2nd September 1951 to its withdrawal on 26th November 1962. In 1952 it was equipped for working iron ore trains from the dock to Consett, a line with some stretches as steep as 1 in 35. The loading was done at a new quay, seen here, provided by Tyne Improvement Commission. Five O1 class were fitted with vacuum brakes for train operation but the pair of 10in. Westinghouse pumps were quite independent. One gave power to hold the wagon bottom doors closed and the other was used for opening the doors with the train on the move at Consett.

British Railways equipped the locomotives and provided set trains of vacuum braked 56 ton bogie wagons with bottom doors operable for discharging at Consett with the train still moving. Here 63856 has one of the eight-wagon train sets on its way to Consett.

6505

Gorton, rebuilt from O4/3.

To traffic 28/4/1945.

REPAIRS:
Gor. 17/5—13/6/47.**G.**
Gor. 31/8—2/9/48.**L.**
Gor. 7—21/5/49.**G.**
Gor. 28/11—22/12/51.**G.**
Gor. 8/10—29/11/52.**C/L.**
Gor. 25/2—26/3/54.**G.**
Gor. 29/12/54—8/1/55.**L.**
Gor. 28/4—21/5/55.**L.**
Gor. 17/5—7/7/56.**G.**
Gor. 20/6—9/8/58.**G.**
Gor. 2—10/6/59.**C/L.**
Gor. 30/7—18/8/59.**C/H.**
Gor. 5/9—14/10/61.**G.**
AWS fitted.

BOILERS:
5034.
5030 *(ex3619)* 13/6/47.
5086 *(ex3777)* 21/5/49.
28366 *(ex63879)* 22/12/51.
28375 *(ex63901)* 26/3/54.
28851 *(ex63868)* 7/7/56.
28971 *(new)* 9/8/58.
28311 *(exO4/8 63606)* 14/10/61.

SHEDS:
Langwith Jct. 28/4/45.
Gorton 29/4/45
Colwick 18/8/46.
Gorton 20/10/46.
Annesley 20/10/50.
March 10/2/57.

RENUMBERED:
3780 30/6/46.
63780 4/9/48.

CONDEMNED: 7/7/63.
Into Don. for cut up 13/8/63.

6507

Gorton, rebuilt from O4/3.

To traffic 24/6/1944.

REPAIRS:
Gor. 21/10/44.**N/C.**
Gor. 17/8—7/9/46.**G.**
Gor. 28/2—13/3/48.**N/C.**
Gor. 3/7—7/8/48.**G.**
Gor. 23/12/50—13/1/51.**G.**
Gor. 1—22/11/52.**G.**
Gor. 16/10—20/11/54.**G.**
Gor. 16/4/55.**N/C.**
Gor. 5—26/1/57.**G.**
Gor. 24/9—29/10/60.**H/I.**

Gor. 29/4—27/5/61.**C/H.**

BOILERS:
5004.
5020 *(ex6350)* 7/9/46.
5115 *(new)* 7/8/48.
28284 *(exB1 61019)* 13/1/51.
28275 *(ex63867)* 22/11/52.
28386 *(ex63591)* 20/11/54.
28829 *(ex63591)* 26/1/57.

SHEDS:
Mexborough 24/6/44.
Gorton 20/8/44.
Annesley 26/11/50.
March 26/5/57.
Staveley 6/12/59.

RENUMBERED:
3784 7/7/46.
E3784 13/3/48.
63784 7/8/48.

CONDEMNED: 29/8/63.
Into Don. for cut up 3/12/63.

6515

Gorton, rebuilt from O4/3.

To traffic 18/11/1944.

REPAIRS:
Gor. 1/2—8/3/47.**G.**
Gor. 15/1—12/2/49.**G.**
S/C smokebox fitted.
Gor. 29/4—6/5/50.**C/L.**
Gor. 25/8—22/9/51.**G.**
Gor. 19/9—3/10/53.**G.**
Gor. 30/10—20/11/54.**C/L.**
Gor. 6/8—10/9/55.**G.**
Gor. 4—11/2/56.**C/L.**
Gor. 24/8—14/9/57.**G.**
Gor. 16/1—20/2/60.**H/I.**
Gor. 6—13/8/60.**C/L.**
Gor. 23/9—7/10/61.**C/L.**
Don. 29/5—14/7/62.**C/H.**

BOILERS:
5012.
5098 *(new)* 8/3/47.
5018 *(ex3879)* 12/2/49.
28345 *(ex63796)* 22/9/51.
28812 *(ex63689)* 3/10/53.
28367 *(ex63678)* 10/9/55.
28132 *(ex63777)* 14/9/57.
28234 *(exB1 61233)* 14/7/62.

SHEDS:
Frodingham 18/11/44.
Gorton 6/12/44.
Annesley 27/10/50.
March 3/3/57.
Staveley 16/9/62.

RENUMBERED:
3786 14/7/46.
63786 12/2/49.

CONDEMNED: 27/9/64.
*Sold for scrap to T.W.Ward,
Killamarsh, 11/64.*

6216

Gorton, rebuilt from O4/1.

To traffic 19/1/1946.

REPAIRS:
Gor. ?/?—?/4/46.**L.**
Drop grate fitted.
Gor. 14/3—3/5/48.**G.**
Gor. 21/6—1/7/48.**N/C.**
Gor. 6/2—12/3/51.**G.**
Gor. 30/3—2/5/52.**C/H.**
Gor. 23/4—16/5/53.**L/I.**
Gor. 2/9—16/10/54.**C/L.**
Gor. 21/4—27/5/55.**G.**
Gor. 20/5—22/6/57.**G.**
Gor. 16/6—10/7/59.**H/I.**
Gor. 30/11—28/12/60.**C/L.**
Gor. 19/5—1/7/61.**G.**

BOILERS:
5033.
5048 *(ex3652)* 3/5/48.
28298 *(exB1 61256)* 12/3/51.
28379 *(ex63678)* 2/5/52.
28275 *(ex63784)* 27/5/55.
28380 *(ex63652)* 22/6/57.
28939 *(exO4/8 63649)* 1/7/61.

SHEDS:
Mexborough 19/1/46.
Gorton 27/1/46.
Hornsey 2/7/48.
Gorton 22/8/48.
Annesley 26/11/50.

RENUMBERED:
3563 2/12/46.
3789 28/2/47.
63789 1/5/48.

CONDEMNED: 17/11/62.
Into Dby. for cut up 6/63.

6283

Gorton, rebuilt from O4/3.

To traffic 16/9/1944.

REPAIRS:
Gor. 14/8—16/11/46.**G.**
Gor. 20/12/48—5/2/49.**G.**
Gor. 6—30/6/51.**G.**

Gor. 3—10/7/51.**N/C.**
Gor. 7—30/8/52.**C/L.**
Gor. 25/6—1/8/53.**G.**
Gor. 2/5—30/6/55.**G.**
Gor. 2—31/8/57.**G.**
Gor. 9/4—6/5/59.**C/L.**
Gor. 22/11/60—6/1/61.**G.**

BOILERS:
5022.
9432 *(ex3712)* 16/11/46.
9427 *(ex3795)* 5/2/49.
28328 *(exO4/8 63893)* 30/6/51.
28310 *(exO4/8 63893)* 1/8/53.
28393 *(ex63676)* 30/6/55.
28257 *(ex63689)* 31/8/57.
28856 *(ex63856)* 6/1/61.

SHEDS:
Gorton 16/9/44.
March 4/10/44.
Annesley 13/2/49.

RENUMBERED:
3792 2/6/46.
63792 5/2/49.

CONDEMNED: 26/10/62.
Into Dby. for cut up 9/63.

6595

Gorton, rebuilt from O4/3.

To traffic 12/2/1944.

REPAIRS:
Gor. 1/6—27/7/46.**G.**
Gor. 4—18/12/48.**G.**
Gor. 4—18/2/50.**C/L.**
After collision.
Gor. 17/3/51.**C/L.**
Gor. 8/9—6/10/51.**G.**
Gor. 19/9—10/10/53.**G.**
Gor. 20/11—18/12/54.**C/H.**
Gor. 31/12/55—4/2/56.**G.**
Gor. 7/12/57—11/1/58.**G.**
Gor. 18—25/10/58.**C/L.**
Gor. 29/7—9/9/61.**H/I.**
Gor. 16—23/9/61.**N/C.**

BOILERS:
9427.
9430 *(ex3591)* 18/12/48.
28351 *(ex63777)* 6/10/51.
28283 *(ex63806)* 10/10/53.
28806 *(ex63865)* 18/12/54.
28839 *(ex63711)* 4/2/56.
28298 *(ex63803)* 11/1/58.

SHEDS:
West Hartlepool 12/2/44.
Gorton 13/3/44.
Annesley 2/4/50.

March 17/2/57.
Staveley 13/12/59.

RENUMBERED:
3795 7/4/46.
63795 18/12/48.

CONDEMNED: 30/10/63.
Into Don. for cut up 7/2/64.

_____

3796
(ex 6596)

Gorton, rebuilt from O4/3.

To traffic 27/4/1946.

REPAIRS:
Gor. 11/9—16/10/47.**L.**
Gor. 31/10—4/12/48.**G.**
Gor. 2/5—2/6/51.**G.**
Gor. 26/5—5/7/52.**C/H.**
Gor. 5—31/10/53.**G.**
Gor. 26/7—28/8/54.**C/L.**
Gor. 14/12/54—29/1/55.**C/L.**
Gor. 3/12/55—14/1/56.**G.**
Gor. 11/12/57—1/2/58.**G.**
Gor. 30/3—14/5/60.**H/I.**

BOILERS:
5055.
5080 *(ex3886)* 4/12/48.
28322 *(ex63838)* 2/6/51.
28396 *(ex63687)* 31/10/53.
28888 *(new)* 14/1/56.

SHEDS:
Tuxford 27/4/46.
Frodingham 5/5/46.
Gorton 12/5/46.
Colwick 18/8/46.
Gorton 20/10/46.
Annesley 22/10/50.
March 17/2/57.
Annesley 14/4/57.

RENUMBERED:
3796 27/4/46.
63796 4/12/48.

CONDEMNED: 26/10/62.
Into Dby. for cut up 9/63.

_____

6220

Gorton, rebuilt from O4/1.

To traffic 9/6/1945.

REPAIRS:
Gor. 17/5—13/6/47.**G.**
Gor. 17—24/1/48.**N/C.**
Gor. 19/9—15/10/48.**L/I.**
Gor. 25/8—15/10/49.**G.**
Gor. 1—15/3/52.**G.**
Gor. 1—24/10/53.**G.**
Gor. 4—24/12/54.**L.**
Gor. 24/9—22/10/55.**G.**
Gor. 9/11—7/12/57.**G.**
Gor. 12—29/11/58.**H.**
After collision.
Gor. 12/2—3/3/59.**H.**
Gor. 19/4—2/6/61.**G.**
Don. 22/2/63. *Not repaired.*

BOILERS:
5037.
5039 *(ex3630)* 13/6/47.
5026 *(ex3619)* 15/10/49.
28374 *(ex63760)* 15/3/52.
28289 *(ex63589)* 24/10/53.
28298 *(ex63752)* 22/10/55.
28805 *(ex63890)* 7/12/57.
28946 *(exO4/8 63709)* 2/6/61.

SHEDS:
Langwith Jct. 9/6/45.
Gorton 17/6/45.
Colwick 18/8/46.
Gorton 20/10/46.
Annesley 16/7/50.
March 17/2/57.

RENUMBERED:
3567 28/11/46.
3803 17/3/47.
63803 15/10/49.

CONDEMNED: 17/3/63.
Cut up at Doncaster.

_____

6601

Gorton, rebuilt from O4/3.

To traffic 12/8/1944.

REPAIRS:
Gor. 24/6—11/8/46.**G.**
Gor. 17/11—31/12/48.**G.**
Gor. 26/10/50—6/1/51.**G.**
Gor. 10—17/1/51.**N/C.**
Gor. 8—21/4/51.**N/C.**
Gor. 4/3—3/5/52.**C/L.**
Gor. 17/4—9/5/53.**G.**
Gor. 1/6—10/7/54.**C/L.**
Gor. 12/4—21/5/55.**G.**
Gor. 22/2—23/3/57.**G.**
Gor. 18/8—18/9/59.**L/I.**

Gor. 20/1—11/2/61.**C/L.**
Gor. 28/3—15/5/62.**G.**

BOILERS:
5006.
5008 *(ex6578)* 11/8/46.
5051 *(ex3887)* 31/12/48.
28283 *(ex63784)* 6/1/51.
28265 *(ex63591)* 9/5/53.
28838 *(exO4/8 63703)* 21/5/55.
28391 *(ex63589)* 23/3/57.
28459 *(exO4/8 63612)* 15/5/62.

SHEDS:
Doncaster 12/8/44.
Thornton Jct. 30/8/44.
Annesley 23/1/49.

RENUMBERED:
3806 3/8/46.
63806 31/12/48.

CONDEMNED: 21/11/62.
Into Dby. for cut up 10/63.

_____

6519

Gorton, rebuilt from O4/3.

To traffic 10/2/1945.

REPAIRS:
Gor. 3/8—20/9/47.**G.**
Gor. 12—25/9/48.**L.**
Gor. 19/10—12/11/49.**G.**
Gor. 19—21/9/50.**C/L.**
Gor. 31/12/51—23/2/52.**G.**
Gor. 26—27/2/52.**N/C.**
Gor. 13/4—1/5/52.**N/C.**
Gor. 25/2—27/3/54.**G.**
Gor. 8/11—4/12/54.**C/L.**
Gor. 21/2—26/3/55.**C/L.**
Gor. 5/4—12/5/56.**G.**
Gor. 9/1—9/2/57.**C/L.**
Gor. 16/1—21/2/59.**L/I.**
Gor. 7/9—14/10/61.**G.**

BOILERS:
5024.
5043 *(ex3646)* 20/9/47.
5031 *(ex3650)* 12/11/49.
28373 *(ex63869)* 23/2/52.
28362 *(ex63711)* 27/3/54.
28303 *(ex63571)* 12/5/56.
28886 *(exO4/8 63816)* 14/10/61.

SHEDS:
Langwith Jct. 10/2/45.
Gorton 25/2/45.
Colwick 18/8/46.

Gorton 20/10/46.
Annesley 16/7/50.

RENUMBERED:
3808 30/7/46.
63808 12/11/49.

CONDEMNED: 17/11/62.
Into Crw. for cut up 9/63.

_____

6263

Gorton, rebuilt from O4/3.

To traffic 14/4/1945.

REPAIRS:
Gor. 30/9—20/10/45.**L.**
Gor. 12/1—1/3/47.**G.**
Gor. 18—22/1/49.**C/L.**
Gor. 8/6—1/7/49.**G.**
Gor. 15—23/7/49.**N/C.**
Gor. 17/4—12/5/51.**G.**
Gor. 15/4—5/6/52.**C/L.**
Gor. 7—9/6/52.**N/C.**
Gor. 29/12/52—23/1/53.**G.**
Gor. 7—30/1/54.**C/L.**
Gor. 2/12/54—8/1/55.**G.**
Gor. 17/3—20/4/56.**C/L.**
Gor. 11/1—9/2/57.**G.**
Gor. 6/4—1/5/59.**H/I.**
Gor. 25/10—2/12/61.**G.**
Gor. 6—13/12/61.**N/C.**

BOILERS:
5036.
5013 *(ex3869)* 1/3/47.
5082 *(ex3760)* 1/7/49.
28811 *(new)* 12/5/51.
28391 *(ex63650)* 23/1/53.
28388 *(ex63594)* 8/1/55.
28358 *(ex63619)* 9/2/57.
28971 *(ex63780)* 2/12/61.

SHEDS:
Colwick 14/4/45.
Gorton 3/6/45.
Colwick 18/8/46.
Gorton 20/10/46.
Annesley 26/11/50.

RENUMBERED:
3817 20/10/46.
63817 22/1/49.

CONDEMNED: 17/11/62.
Into Crw. for cut up 9/63.

_____

WORKS CODES:- Bpk - Beyer, Peacock. Crw - Crewe. Cw - Cowlairs. Dar- Darlington. Dby - Derby. Don - Doncaster. Ghd - Gateshead. Gor - Gorton. Inv - Inverurie. Str - Stratford.
REPAIR CODES:- **C/H** - Casual Heavy. **C/L** - Casual Light. **G** - General. **H** - Heavy. **H/I** - Heavy Intermediate. **L** - Light. **L/I** - Light Intermediate. **N/C** - Non-Classified.

Consett Ironworks Company provided the special quick discharging facilities which 63856 and its train are here traversing.

63838
(ex 6261/3838)

Gorton, rebuilt from O4/3.

To traffic 4/6/1949.

REPAIRS:
Gor. 28/1—3/3/51.**G.**
Gor. 7—20/3/51.**N/C.**
Gor. 17/3—17/5/52.**C/L.**
Gor. 18/4—16/5/53.**G.**
Gor. 24/3—29/4/55.**G.**
Gor. 16/6—8/7/55.**C/L.**
Gor. 4/5—1/6/57.**G.**
Gor. 28/8—20/9/58.**C/L.**
Gor. 5—28/2/59.**C/H.**
Gor. 16/8—17/9/60.**H/I.**
Gor. 6—31/1/62.**C/L.**
AWS fitted.

BOILERS:
5112.
28297 (ex63806) 3/3/51.
28826 (ex63890) 16/5/53.
28286 (ex63854) 29/4/55.
28350 (ex63752) 1/6/57.

SHEDS:
Staveley 4/6/49.
Annesley 19/6/49.

RENUMBERED:
63838 3/6/49.

CONDEMNED: 26/10/62.
Into Dby. for cut up 10/63.

_____

6526

Gorton, rebuilt from O4/3.

To traffic 7/6/1946.

REPAIRS:
Gor. 30/5—30/6/48.**G.**
Gor. 27/2—28/4/50.**C/L.**
Gor. 10/1—10/2/51.**G.**
Gor. 31/10—22/11/52.**G.**
Gor. 31/5—10/7/54.**C/L.**
Gor. 26/1—3/3/55.**G.**
Gor. 10/11—15/12/56.**C/H.**
Gor. 24/8—28/9/57.**H/I.**
Gor. 2/6—12/7/58.**C/H.**
Gor. 20/5—30/6/61.**H/I.**

BOILERS:
5057.
5047 (ex3768) 30/6/48.
28290 (exB1 61062) 10/2/51.
28286 (ex63865) 22/11/52.
28384 (ex63867) 3/3/55.
28351 (ex63725) 15/12/56.

SHEDS:
Colwick 7/6/46.
Gorton 16/6/46.
Colwick 18/8/46.
Gorton 20/10/46.
Annesley 26/11/50.

RENUMBERED:
3854 12/12/46.
63854 26/6/48.

CONDEMNED: 17/11/62.
Into Crw. for cut up 9/63.

_____

63856
(ex 6617/3856)

Gorton, rebuilt from O4/3.

To traffic 22/10/1949.

REPAIRS:
Gor. 10/8—8/9/51.**G.**
Gor. 18/4—17/5/52.**C/L.**
Westinghouse pumps & vacuum
ejector fitted for iron ore traffic.
Gor. 23/12/53—30/1/54.**G.**
Gor. 26/11/54—22/1/55.**C/L.**
Gor. 19/4—26/5/56.**C/L.**
Gor. 11/10—1/12/56.**G.**
Gor. 26/11/59—1/2/60.**G.**
Dar. 16/11—17/12/60.**C/L.**
Gor. 12/9—21/10/61.**C/L.**

BOILERS:
5120.
28343 (ex63755) 8/9/51.
28335 (ex63886) 30/1/54.
28856 (exO4/8 63721) 1/12/56.
28321 (exO4/8 63645) 1/2/60.

SHEDS:
Hull Dairycoates 22/10/49.
Hull Springhead 5/2/50.
Hull Dairycoates 21/5/50.
Tyne Dock 2/9/51.

RENUMBERED:
63856 22/10/49.

CONDEMNED: 26/11/62.
Into Gor. for cut up 5/63.

_____

6533

Gorton, rebuilt from O4/3.

To traffic 1/9/1945.

REPAIRS:
Gor. 22/11—6/12/47.**G.**
Gor. 6—20/5/50.**G.**
Gor. 21/6—26/7/52.**G.**

Gor. 1—22/8/53.**C/H.**
Gor. 5/6—3/7/54.**G.**
Gor. 30/7—20/8/55.**C/L.**
Gor. 3/11—8/12/56.**G.**
Gor. 22/8—19/9/59.**G.**
Gor. 12/12/59.**N/C.**
Gor. 30/1—6/2/60.**C/L.**
Don. 31/10—14/12/62.**G.**

BOILERS:
5042.
5114 (new) 6/12/47.
5052 (ex63687) 20/5/50.
28383 (ex63579) 26/7/52.
28366 (ex63780) 3/7/54.
28363 (ex63590) 8/12/56.
28983 (new) 19/9/59.
28202 (exB1 61111) 14/12/62.

SHEDS:
Doncaster 1/9/45.
Gorton 9/9/45.
Colwick 18/8/46.
Gorton 20/10/46.
Annesley 16/7/50.
Colwick 3/11/57.
Staveley 9/6/63.
Barrow Hill 13/6/65.

RENUMBERED:
3863 7/7/46.
63863 20/5/50.

CONDEMNED: 20/6/65.
Sold for scrap to R.A.King,
Norwich 8/65.

_____

6535

Gorton, rebuilt from O4/3.

To traffic 9/2/1946.

REPAIRS:
Gor. ?/?—?/?/46.**N/C.**
Drop grate fitted.
Gor. 17/1—23/2/48.**G.**
Gor. 15/7—10/8/50.**G.**
Gor. 9/12/50—13/1/51.**C/L.**
Gor. 18/8—13/9/52.**G.**
Gor. 16/10—14/11/53.**C/L.**
Gor. 4/10—13/11/54.**G.**
Gor. 28/12/55—28/1/56.**C/L.**
Gor. 12/11—14/12/56.**G.**
Gor. 10/3—10/4/59.**L/I.**
Gor. 19/8—23/9/61.**G.**

BOILERS:
5049.
5044 (ex3578) 23/2/48.
5040 (ex63670) 10//8/50.
5040 reno.28286 13/1/51.
28806 (ex63592) 13/9/52.
28299 (ex63652) 13/11/54.

28383 (ex63746) 14/12/56.
28118 (ex63874) 23/9/61.

SHEDS:
Doncaster 9/2/46.
Gorton 17/2/46.
New England 23/5/48.
Gorton 14/7/48.
Annesley 26/11/50.

RENUMBERED:
3865 7/7/46.
ᴇ**3865** 23/2/48.
63865 10/8/50.

CONDEMNED: 17/11/62.
Into Crw. for cut up 9/63.

_____

6624

Gorton, rebuilt from O4/3.

To traffic 2/9/1944.

REPAIRS:
Gor. 2/6—27/7/46.**G.**
Gor. 20/8—2/10/48.**G.**
Gor. 20/10—25/11/50.**G.**
Gor. 23/8—20/9/52.**G.**
Gor. 18/10—20/11/54.**G.**
Gor. 12—21/5/55.**N/C.**
Gor. 18/1—16/2/57.**G.**
Gor. 11/3—10/4/59.**G.**
Gor. 29/12/59—15/1/60.**C/L.**
Gor. 10/11—9/12/61.**L/I.**
Gor. 28/12/61.**N/C.**
Gor. 23/5—28/6/62.**C/L.**

BOILERS:
5007.
9436 (ex6630) 27/7/46.
5020 (ex3784) 2/10/48.
28275 (ex63746) 25/11/50.
28384 (exO4/8 63882) 20/9/52.
28390 (ex63773) 20/11/54.
28362 (ex63808) 16/2/57.
28381 (exO4/8 63703) 10/4/59.

SHEDS:
Doncaster 2/9/44.
March 28/9/44.
Annesley 31/1/49.

RENUMBERED:
3867 2/6/46.
63867 2/10/48.

CONDEMNED: 17/11/62.
Into Crw. for cut up 8/63.

_____

6625

Gorton, rebuilt from O4/3.

To traffic 24/2/1945.

REPAIRS:
Gor. 19/4—17/5/47.**G.**
Gor. 5—26/11/49.**G.**
Gor. 24/3—21/4/51.**C/H.**
Gor. 17—31/5/52.**G.**
Gor. 16—30/5/53.**C/L.**
Gor. 3/4—1/5/54.**G.**
Gor. 4—25/6/55.**C/L.**
Gor. 24/3—28/4/56.**G.**
Gor. 22/2—15/3/58.**G.**
Gor. 2/9—14/10/61.**H/I.**
AWS fitted.
Don. 25/2—29/3/63.**C/H.**

BOILERS:
5026.
5012 *(ex3786)* 17/5/47.
5039 *(ex3803)* 26/11/49.
5039 reno.28307 21/4/51.
28829 *(new)* 31/5/52.
28851 *(new)* 1/5/54.
28332 *(ex63596)* 28/4/56.
28297 *(ex63890)* 15/3/58.
28527 *(exB1 61329)* 29/3/63.

SHEDS:
Gorton 24/2/45.
Woodford 18/8/46.
Gorton 20/10/46.
Annesley 2/7/50.
March 17/2/57.
Staveley 24/2/63.
Langwith Jct. 13/6/65.

RENUMBERED:
3868 7/4/46.
63868 26/11/49.

CONDEMNED: 11/7/65.
Sold for scrap to A.Draper,
Hull, 8/65. Cut up 1/11/65.

6626

Gorton, rebuilt from O4/3.

To traffic 2/12/1944.

REPAIRS:
Gor. 22/12/46—8/2/47.**G.**
Gor. 27/4—20/6/47.**L.**
Gor. 29/5—8/6/48.**L.**
Gor. 26/9—22/10/49.**G.**
Gor. 29/11/51—5/1/52.**G.**
Gor. 20/1—19/2/53.**C/L.**
Gor. 29/10—14/11/53.**G.**
Gor. 27/1—3/3/55.**C/L.**
Gor. 28/6—6/8/55.**C/H.**

Gor. 9/2—16/3/56.**L/I.**
Gor. 12/3—12/4/58.**G.**
Gor. 16—20/12/58.**N/C.**
Gor. 19/8—23/9/61.**H/I.**

BOILERS:
5013.
5010 *(ex3879)* 8/2/47.
5081 *(ex3725)* 22/10/49.
28369 *(exO4/8 63827)* 5/1/52.
28359 *(ex63879)* 14/11/53.
28290 *(ex63890)* 6/8/55.
28325 *(ex63711)* 12/4/58.

SHEDS:
Doncaster 2/12/44.
Gorton 10/12/44.
Colwick 18/8/46.
Gorton 20/10/46.
Annesley 2/7/50.

RENUMBERED:
3869 6/4/46.
63869 8/6/48.

CONDEMNED: 17/11/62.
Into Crw. for cut up 8/63.

3872
(ex 6525)

Gorton, rebuilt from O4/3.

To traffic 18/5/1946.

REPAIRS:
Gor. ?/?—?/8/46.**N/C.**
Drop grate fitted.
Gor. 20/3—17/4/48.**G.**
Gor. 5—19/8/50.**G.**
Gor. 28/7—18/8/51.**C/H.**
Gor. 6—20/12/52.**G.**
Gor. 6/11—4/12/54.**G.**
Gor. 9/4/55.**N/C.**
Gor. 24/11—22/12/56.**G.**
Gor. 19/9—17/10/59.**L/I.**
Don. 1/2—30/3/62.**G.**

BOILERS:
5056.
5045 *(ex3901)* 17/4/48.
5111 *(ex63594)* 19/8/50.
5111 reno.28336 18/8/51.
28387 *(ex63663)* 20/12/52.
28329 *(ex63768)* 4/12/54.
28924 *(new)* 22/12/56.

SHEDS:
Frodingham 18/5/46.
Gorton 26/5/46.
Colwick 18/8/46.
Gorton 20/10/46.
Hornsey 2/7/48.
Gorton 5/9/48.

Annesley 26/11/50.
March 26/5/57.
Staveley 24/11/63.

RENUMBERED:
3872 18/5/46.
63872 17/4/48.

CONDEMNED: 30/1/64.
Sold for scrap to T.W.Ward,
Beighton, 4/64.

6630

Gorton, rebuilt from O4/3.

To traffic 10/6/1944.

REPAIRS:
Gor. 27/5—22/6/46.**G.**
Gor. 2—26/2/49.**G.**
Gor. 24/6—29/7/49.**C/L.**
After collision.
Gor. 5/5—2/6/51.**G.**
Gor. 5/8—18/10/52.**C/L.**
Vacuum ejector & Westinghouse
pumps fitted for iron ore traffic.
Gor. 26/2—27/3/54.**G.**
Gor. 19/6—25/8/56.**G.**
Ghd. 27/5—20/6/58.**C/L.**
Gor. 27/5—3/7/59.**H/I.**
Gor. 19/4—4/6/60.**C/L.**
Gor. 9/5—2/8/61.**C/H.**
Gor. 12/8—2/9/61.**N/C.**
Gor. 31/10—30/11/61.**N/C.**
Dar. 11—21/5/62.**C/L.**

BOILERS:
9436.
5083 *(new)* 22/6/46.
9432 *(ex3792)* 26/2/49.
28323 *(exO4/8 63828)* 2/6/51.
28825 *(ex63579)* 27/3/54.
28118 *(exO4/8 63893)* 25/8/56.
28365 *(exO4/8 63647)* 2/8/61.

SHEDS:
Heaton 10/6/44.
Tyne Dock 19/10/44
Hull Springhead 18/6/45.
Tyne Dock 15/6/46.
Darlington 6/2/49.
Hull Dairycoates 11/9/49.
Hull Springhead 5/2/50.
Hull Dairycoates 21/5/50.
Tyne Dock 2/9/51.

RENUMBERED:
3874 22/6/46.
63874 26/2/49.

CONDEMNED: 26/11/62.
Into Gor. for cut up 1/63.

6288

Gorton, rebuilt from O4/2.

To traffic 4/11/1944.

REPAIRS:
Gor. 28/12/46—1/2/47.**G.**
Gor. 12/12/48—8/1/49.**G.**
Gor. 20/10—17/11/51.**G.**
Tender fitted for Alfloc briquettes.
Gor. 26/9—17/10/53.**G.**
Gor. 8—22/5/54.**C/L.**
Gor. 11/12/54.**C/L.**
Gor. 26/3—14/5/55.**C/L.**
Gor. 25/2—24/3/56.**G.**
Gor. 11/8—15/9/56.**C/L.**
Gor. 4/1—1/2/58.**C/L.**
Gor. 20/12/58—24/1/59.**G.**
Don. 15/6—22/8/62.**G.**

BOILERS:
5010.
5018 *(ex5408)* 1/2/47.
5055 *(ex3796)* 8/1/49.
28359 *(ex63610)* 17/11/51.
28328 *(ex63792)* 17/10/53.
28345 *(ex63886)* 24/3/56.
28828 *(ex63746)* 24/1/59.
28500 *(exB1 61153)* 22/8/62.

SHEDS:
Annesley 4/11/44.
Gorton 3/12/44.
Colwick 18/8/46.
Gorton 20/10/46.
Annesley 23/4/50.
March 10/2/57.
Staveley 24/11/63.
Barrow Hill 13/6/65.

RENUMBERED:
3879 2/6/46.
63879 8/1/49.

CONDEMNED: 11/7/65.
Sold for scrap to A.Draper,
Hull, 8/65. Cut up 27/9/65.

3886
(ex 6635)

Gorton, rebuilt from O4/3.

To traffic 3/8/1946.

REPAIRS:
Gor. 3/10—6/11/48.**G.**
Gor. 18/6—4/8/51.**G.**
Gor. 7—9/8/51.**N/C.**
Gor. 27/9—3/11/51.**C/L.**
Gor. 22/9—24/10/52.**C/L.**
Gor. 23/10—14/11/53.**G.**
Gor. 8/8—24/9/55.**G.**

63874 was another of the five fitted in 1952 for these special block workings. The other three were 63712, 63755 and 63760. Until 1956 they worked as the train engines but from 18th May that year, BR Standard 9F 2-10-0 engines gradually took over this working.

63755, after being deprived of leading these heavy trains, could still be usefully employed in banking them as here at Beamish.

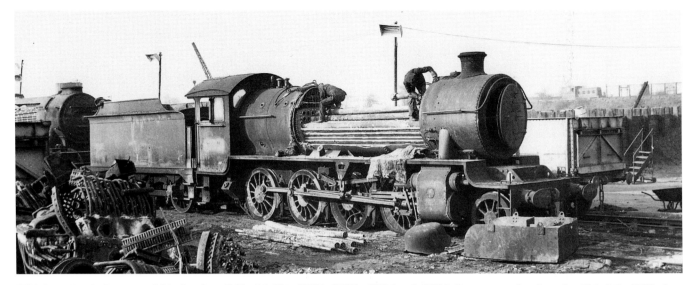

Withdrawal only began on 26th October 1962 with Nos.63777, 63792, 63796 and 63838. It was completed on the 11th July 1965 when the last seven, Nos.63589, 63590, 63630, 63646, 63725, 63768 and 63868 were taken out of stock. No.63571 was sold to Albert Draper & Son for scrap at an earlier date and is seen in their scrap yard at Hull on 29th March 1965 being dismantled.

3886 continued.
Gor. 9/5—8/6/57.**G.**
Gor. 28/5—14/6/58.**C/L.**
Gor. 1—30/8/58.**C/L.**
Gor. 18/2—23/3/60.**H/I.**

BOILERS:
 5080.
 5057 *(ex3854)* 6/11/48.
 28335 *(ex63887)* 4/8/51.
 28345 *(ex63786)* 14/11/53.
 28812 *(ex63786)* 24/9/55.
 28838 *(ex63806)* 8/6/57.

SHEDS:
Woodford 3/8/46.
Gorton 4/8/46.
Annesley 22/10/50.

RENUMBERED:
 3886 3/8/46.
 63886 6/11/48.

CONDEMNED: 26/10/62.
Into Crw. for cut up 9/63.
_____

6636

Gorton, rebuilt from O4/3.

To traffic 2/3/1946.

REPAIRS:
Gor. ?/?—?/4/46.**N/C.**
Drop grate fitted.
Gor. 25/7—4/9/48.**G.**
Gor. 7/5—16/6/51.**G.**
Gor. 11/3—11/4/53.**G.**
Gor. 12/7—28/8/54.**C/L.**
Gor. 31/8—2/9/54.**N/C.**
Gor. 20/8—30/11/55.**G.**

Gor. 31/7—1/9/56.**C/L.**
Gor. 15/1—23/2/57.**C/L.**
Gor. 31/10—23/11/57.**G.**
Gor. 26/11—25/12/57.**N/C.**
Gor. 1/10—9/11/60.**G.**
Don. 15/2/63. *Not repaired.*

BOILERS:
 5051.
 5085 *(ex3592)* 4/9/48.
 28809 *(new)* 16/6/51.
 28336 *(ex63872)* 11/4/53.
 28824 *(ex63592)* 30/11/55.
 28283 *(ex63663)* 23/11/57.

SHEDS:
Frodingham 2/3/46.
Gorton 12/5/46.
Woodford 18/8/46.
Gorton 20/10/46.
Annesley 26/11/50.
March 14/4/57
Staveley 16/9/62.

RENUMBERED:
 3887 23/6/46.
 63887 4/9/48.

CONDEMNED: 2/3/63.
Cut up at Doncaster.
_____

3890
(ex 6639)

Gorton, rebuilt from O4/3.

To traffic 6/7/1946.

REPAIRS:
Gor. ?/?—?/1/47.**N/C.**
Drop grate fitted.

Gor. 27/5—26/6/48.**G.**
Gor. 23/12/50—13/1/51.**G.**
Gor. 24/1—23/2/52.**G.**
Gor. 24/1—14/2/53.**G.**
Gor. 18/9—23/10/54.**G.**
Gor. 15/6—30/7/55.**H/I.**
Gor. 8/5—16/6/56.**G.**
Gor. 23/2—9/3/57.**C/L.**
Gor. 14/12/57—11/1/58.**G.**
Gor. 10/12/60—21/1/61.**H/I.**
Gor. 16/12/61—3/2/62.**C/L.**
AWS fitted.

BOILERS:
 5079.
 5049 *(ex3865)* 26/6/48.
 28805 *(new)* 13/1/51.
 28826 *(new)* 23/2/52.
 28290 *(ex63854)* 14/2/53.
 28805 *(ex63687)* 23/10/54.
 28297 *(ex63646)* 16/6/56.
 28367 *(ex63786)* 11/1/58.

SHEDS:
Staveley 6/7/46.
Gorton 14/7/46.
Woodford 18/8/46.
Gorton 20/10/46.
Annesley 26/11/50.
March 14/4/57.

RENUMBERED:
 3890 6/7/46.
 63890 26/6/48.

CONDEMNED: 17/3/63.
Into Don. for cut up 27/3/63.
_____

6642

Gorton, rebuilt from O4/3.

To traffic 27/10/1945.

REPAIRS:
Gor. ?/?—?/2/46.**N/C.**
Drop grate fitted.
Gor. 20/6—17/8/46.**L.**
Gor. 11/11—21/12/47.**G.**
Gor. 10/1—4/2/50.**G.**
Gor. 7—13/2/50.**N/C.**
Gor. 20/2—5/4/52.**G.**
Gor. 4/7—9/8/52.**C/L.**
Gor. 8/1—3/2/54.**G.**
Gor. 7/1—12/2/55.**C/L.**
Gor. 13/1—18/2/56.**G.**
Gor. 14/4—17/5/58.**G.**
Gor. 11/10—25/11/61.**L/I.**

BOILERS:
 5045.
 5024 *(ex3808)* 21/12/47.
 5012 *(ex3868)* 4/2/50.
 28375 *(ex63619)* 5/4/52.
 28372 *(ex63650)* 3/2/54.
 28396 *(ex63796)* 18/2/56.
 28373 *(exO4/8 63827)* 17/5/58.

SHEDS:
Frodingham 27/10/45.
Gorton 4/11/45.
Annesley 2/7/50.

RENUMBERED:
 3901 7/4/46.
 63901 4/2/50.

CONDEMNED: 17/11/62.
Into Crw. for cut up 8/63.
_____

YEADON'S REGISTER OF LNER LOCOMOTIVES - Volumes 1 to 29

Vol.1
Gresley A1 &
A3 class.
Reprint

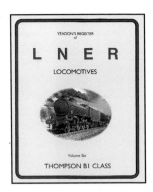

Vol.6
The
Thompson
B1's.
Reprint

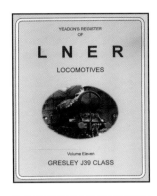

Vol.11
The J39
Class

Vol.2
The Gresley
A4's.
Reprint

Vol.7
The B12's.
Reprint

Vol.12
Steam
Railcars &
Sentinel
Locos

Vol.3
The Raven,
Thompson &
Peppercorn
Pacifc's.
Reprint

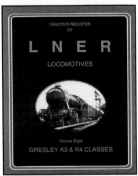

Vol.8
The Gresley
K3's.
Reprint

Vol.13
C1, C2, C4 &
C5 Atlantic
Tender
Engines

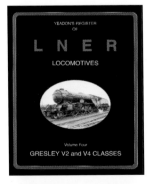

Vol.4
The Gresley
V2 & V4
classes.
Reprint

Vol.9
The Gresley
Eight-
Coupled
engines.
Reprint

Vol.14
D13, D14,
D15 & D16 -
The GER
4-4-0's

Vol.5
The Gresley
B17's &
Thompson
B2's.
Reprint

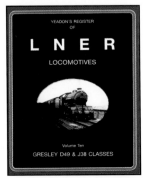

Vol.10
The D49 &
J38 classes.
Reprint

Vol.15
The J94, O6
& O7 classes